Review and Test Preparation Guide
for the Beginning Latin Student

Review and Test Preparation Guide

for the Beginning Latin Student

Thalia Pantelidis Hocker

Addison-Wesley Publishing Company
Reading, Massachusetts • Menlo Park, California • New York
Don Mills, Ontario • Wokingham, England • Amsterdam • Bonn
Sydney • Singapore • Tokyo • Madrid • San Juan • Paris
Seoul, Korea • Milan • Mexico City • Taipei, Taiwan

Review and Test Preparation Guide for the Beginning Latin Student
Copyright © 1995 by Addison-Wesley Publishing Company, Inc.
All rights reserved.
No paft of this publication may be reproduced,
stored in a retrieval system, or transmitted
in any form or by any means, electronic, mechanical,
photocopying, recording, or otherwise,
without the prior permission of the publisher.

A publication of World Language Division

Executive editor: Lyn McLean
Production: Karen Philippidis, Nik Winter
Text design: Curt Belshe
Cover design: Woodshed Productions
Cover illustration: Courtesy of Elizabeth Lyding Will
Text art: Woodshed Productions

ISBN: 0-8013-1195-0

1 2 3 4 5 6 7 8 9 10-CRS-989769594

CONTENTS

Preface

I have never met a Latin teacher who thought that the basal text that he or she was using was perfect. We have all wished that our basal text contained more exercises and reading drills for practice and review. Or we may have wished for a way to expose our students to different Latin vocabulary. Who in September has not faced the laborious task of writing review worksheets for our second year classes? (How is it that our students over the summer seem to have forgotten everything we ever taught them about Latin?) *Review and Test Preparation Guide for the Beginning Latin Student* has been designed to meet these needs. The workbook provides varied and innovative supplementary grammar review exercises for any type of beginning Latin program on both the secondary and college level. Grammar is reviewed in small enough segments that the practice exercises can be used as additional practice of a particular grammar item currently being taught or as a general review of grammar before final exams or at the beginning of the following school year.

Wherever possible, I have tried to present grammar material in the context of a sentence or story. Throughout the book there are clear, concise, easy to understand grammar explanations with helpful charts and mnemonic devices. Exercises dealing with just isolated grammatical forms have been kept to a minimum. I think that students will particularly enjoy the "picture" exercises in Part One of the workbook. Many exercises employ a multiple choice format similar to that used in JCL competitions, the National Latin Exam, and other standardized tests. I have placed a major emphasis on reading for comprehension and not on translating English sentences into Latin. The vocabulary used is reflective of the major changes in the Latin curriculum used today. There is much less emphasis on "war" words and more emphasis on vocabulary pertaining to everyday life.

The exercises are varied in their level of difficulty. The workbook can be used for remedial purposes with a student who is having difficulty mastering Latin grammar. Yet the format and content of the book also provides the students who excel in Latin the opportunity to work ahead on their own.

Not even this workbook is "perfect." However, I hope that you will find some requests from your wish list fulfilled on the pages that follow.

Thalia Pantelidis Hocker

Thalia Pantelidis Hocker, the author of this Review Book, and Sally Davis, the author of the companion Intermediate Review Book, both acknowledge the invaluable suggestions, corrections and encouragement of Ron Palma of Holland Hall School, Tulsa, Oklahoma.

MEO DULCISSIMO CONIUGI

P A R T 1
....
Nouns and Case Uses
CHAPTER I — THE NOMINATIVE AND ACCUSATIVE CASES

HOW NOUNS ARE DECLINED

When translating nouns in a Latin sentence, you must consider four important facts about each noun:

1) **Case** - the ending of a noun that defines its function or use in a sentence.
   Pōnite cistās in raedā.   *Place the trunks in the wagon.*

   The case ending **-ās** lets us know that the noun **cistās** is the direct object of this sentence.

2) **Gender** - refers to whether a noun is considered *masculine*, *feminine*, or *neuter*. Nouns of the first declension are *feminine* with just a few exceptions. Nouns of the second declension are either *masculine* or *neuter*. Nouns of the third declension may be *masculine*, *feminine* or *neuter*.
   Raeda (f) est magna.   *The wagon is large.*
   Hortus (m) est magnus.   *The garden is large.*
   Flūmen (n) est magnum.   *The river is large.*

3) **Number** - refers to whether a noun is *singular* or *plural*.
   Senātor est occupātus.   *The senator is busy.*
   Senatōrēs sunt occupātī.   *The senators are busy.*

4) **Declension** - refers to the family to which a noun belongs. An ending such as **-a** can have a different meaning depending on the declension of the noun.
   Puella (1st declen.) est pulchra.   *The girl is beautiful.*
   Aedificia (2nd declen.) sunt pulchra.   *The buildings are beautiful.*

We will begin with the *Nominative* and *Accusative* forms of *masculine* and *feminine* nouns of the 1st, 2nd, and 3rd declensions. Look at the chart below:

CASE	1st Declension	2nd Declension	3rd Declension
SING.			
Nom.	fābul**a**	hort**us**	senātor
Acc.	fābul**am**	hort**um**	senātor**em**
PL.			
Nom.	fābul**ae**	hort**ī**	senātor **ēs**
Acc.	fābul **ās**	hort**ōs**	senātor **ēs**

NOTA BENE:

While most nouns of the first declension are feminine, the names of certain occupations are masculine.

Second declension nouns are mostly masculine but there are also some neuter nouns.

The third declension contains nouns that are masculine, feminine , or neuter.

The Accusative Singular of all three declensions ends in **-m**.

The Accusative Plural of all three declensions ends in **-s**.

The Nominative Singular of the third declension is variable: **senātor, homō.**

The Nominative and Accusative Plural of third declension nouns are identical.

From the context of the sentence you can decide whether such nouns are Nominative or Accusative.

PRACTICE ONE

On a separate sheet of paper, complete noun declension charts for the following nouns. Use the noun declension chart above as your guide.

1st Declension	2nd Declension	3rd Declension
1. familia	3. rāmus	5. homō, hominis
2. agricola	4. vir	6. lēx, lēgis

PRACTICE TWO

Write **Nom** *next to the noun forms that are nominative. Write* **Acc** *next to the noun forms that are accusative. Write* **N or A** *next to the noun forms that could be either case.*

1.	puellam	_____	6. vōcēs	_____	11. servī	_____
2.	virum	_____	7. senātōrem	_____	12. vīlicus	_____
3.	mūrem	_____	8. agrī	_____	13. fragōrem	_____
4.	rēx	_____	9. rāmōs	_____	14. pīctūrae	_____
5.	īnsula	_____	10. equī	_____	15. nāvēs	_____

HOW THE NOMINATIVE AND ACCUSATIVE CASES ARE USED IN LATIN

THE NOMINATIVE CASE

1) **Subject** - the person or object that is performing the action in the sentence.
    Puella in agrīs ambulat.   *The **girl** walks in the fields.*

2) **Predicate** - redefines or renames the subject of the sentence. A sentence that has a form of the verb *to be* (**sum, esse**) as its main verb will often contain a *predicate*.
    Antōnia est **mea amīca**.   *Antonia is **my friend**.*

THE ACCUSATIVE CASE

1) **Direct object** - the person or object that receives the action of the verb.
    Puella novam **stolam** gerit.   *The girl wears **a new dress**.*

PRACTICE THREE

Look at the picture and circle the Latin sentence that accurately describes the picture.

1. a. Canēs puerum latrant.
   b. Canēs puer latrat.
   c. Canis puerōs latrat.

2. a. Puella est laeta.
   b. Puellae sunt laetae.
   c. Puellae sunt īrātae.

3. a. Epistula patrem scrībit.
   b. Epistulam pater scrībit.
   c. Epistulās patrēs scrībunt.

4. a. Mīlitem senātor salūtat.
   b. Mīles senatōrēs salūtat.
   c. Mīlitēs senatōrem salūtant.

5. a. Coquus cēnam parat.
   b. Coqui cēnam parant.
   c. Coquum cēna parat.

6. a. Servus dēfessus dormit.
   b. Servī dēfessī dormiunt.
   c. Servus strēnuus currit.

PRACTICE FOUR

*Indicate whether the underlined noun or pronoun in each sentence would be in the Nom or Acc Case in Latin.   Also indicate whether the noun is **singular** or **plural**.*

	Case	Number
1. Antonius has two <u>sisters</u>.	_____	_____
2. The name of one of his sisters is <u>Antonia.</u>	_____	_____
3. Antonius has a <u>friend</u> named Rufus.	_____	_____
4. The <u>boys</u> often play in the fields.	_____	_____
5. Antonius puts on a new <u>tunic</u>.	_____	_____
6. Then <u>he</u> walks with Rufus to the forum.	_____	_____
7. Next the boys visit the <u>Circus</u>.	_____	_____
8. Flavius does not often hit his <u>slaves</u>.	_____	_____
9. The slave still fears Flavius' <u>stick</u>.	_____	_____
10 Flavius asks, "Slave, where are your <u>tools</u>?"	_____	_____

PRACTICE FIVE

Circle each noun that is a Subject or Predicate. Underline each noun that is a Direct Object. Then translate each sentence into English.

1. Lūcius puellās videt._____

2. Puellae Lūcium vexant._____

3. Puer et puellae lupōs vident._____

4. Lupī puerum terrent sed nōn puellās._____

5. Nūntius epistulās fert._____

6. Epistulās pater Lūciī legit._____

7. Prīnceps senatōrēs revocat._____

8. Claudia est puella Rōmāna._____

9. Pater Claudiae puerōs et puellam salūtat._____

10. Puerī et puella patrem et mātrem salūtant._____

11. Puellae poētam petunt._____

12. Poēta multōs librōs habet._____

13. Puellae multās fābulās poētae audiunt._____

14. Nunc puellae sunt laetae._____

PRACTICE SIX

Select the correct form of the noun to complete the meaning of the sentence and place the letter of your answer in the space provided.

_____ 1. Lūcius et Antōnius sunt _____ .   a. puerī   b. puerōs   c. puer

_____ 2. Puerī _____ multās ascendunt.   a. arbor   b. arborēs   c. arborem

_____ 3. Puerī magnam_____audiunt.   a. vōx   b. vōcēs   c. vōcem

_____ 4. _____ Lucius videt.   a. Servus   b. Servōs   c. Servī

_____ 5. Sunt _____ multī in Ītaliā.   a. servī   b. servōs   c. servus

_____ 6. _____ epistulās scrībit.   a. Pater   b. Patrēs   c. Patrem

_____ 7. _____ epistulās Rōmam fert.   a. Nūntiōs   b. Nūntius   c. Nūntium

_____ 8. Nūntius_____ clārum salūtat.   a. senātor   b. senātōris   c. senātōrem

_____ 9. Senātor_____ legit.   a. epistulae   b. epistula   c. epistulās

___ 10. Rufus est_____ Rōmānus.   a. puerum   b. puerōs   c. puer

___ 11. Rufus omnēs _____cōnspicit.   a. mīles   b. mīlitēs   c. mīlitem

___ 12. Mīlitēs _____ salūtant.   a. puerum   b. puerī   c. puer

PRACTICE SEVEN

Make each sentence say the opposite and make all necessary changes. Translate the new sentence into English. The first one is done for you.

1. Mīlitēs incolam spectant. <u>Mīlitēs incola spectat.</u>

   <u>The inhabitant watches the soldiers.</u>

2. Senātōrēs aurīgās vident._____

   _____

3. Frāter amīcam terret._____

   _____

4. Pater puerum audit._____

   _____

5. Dominus servōs petit._____

   _____

6. Agricola servōs cōnspicit._____

   _____

7. Magister discipulōs invenit._____

_____

8. Pīrāta mīlitēs videt._____

_____

9. Virī senatōrem salūtant._____

_____

10. Māter fīliās amat._____

_____

PRACTICE EIGHT

Fill in the blanks with the Nominative or Accusative ending required by the sense of the sentence.

1. Claudia et Antōnia Lūci_____vident.

2. Puell_____ sunt laetae.

3. Patr_____ fīliī saepe vexant.

4. Pat_____ fīliōs amant.

5. Rēgem popul_____ salūtat.

6. Rēgīn_____ sed nōn rēg_____ amō.

7. Pīrāt_____nautās terrent.

8. Pīrātae multōs captīv_____ habent.

9. Senatōrēs nāv_____ vīsitant.

10. Pulchra est nāv_____ .

CHAPTER II — THE NOMINATIVE AND ACCUSATIVE CASES OF NEUTER NOUNS

· ·

NEUTER NOUNS

In this chapter we will review the Nominative and Accusative forms of neuter nouns. Look at the chart below:

CASE	2nd Declension	3rd Declension	3rd Declension
SING.			
Nom.	baculum	corpus	nōmen
Acc.	baculum	corpus	nōmen
PL.			
Nom.	bacula	corpora	nōmina
Acc.	bacula	corpora	nōmina

NOTA BENE:

Both 2nd and 3rd declensions contain neuter nouns. There are no neuter nouns in the 1st declension.

Neuter nouns have endings identical to their masculine and feminine counterparts except in the Nominative and Accusative Cases.

The Nominative Singular form of a 2nd declension noun ends in **-um.**

The Nominative and Accusative forms of a neuter noun are always identical.

For both the 2nd and 3rd declensions the Nominative and Accusative neuter plural forms end in **-a.**

PRACTICE ONE

On a separate sheet of paper, complete noun declension charts for the following neuter nouns. Use the noun declension chart above as your guide.

2nd Declension

1. perīculum
2. verbum
3. gaudium

3rd Declension

4. lītus, lītōris
5. caput, capitis
6. iter, itineris

PRACTICE TWO

Check whether the underlined word is in the Nominative or Accusative Case as it is used in the sentence. Then translate each sentence into English.

	Nom.	Acc.
1. Ubī vōs Rōmam <u>iter</u> facere potestis?	_____	_____
2. Sunt magna <u>perīcula</u> in urbe.	_____	_____
3. Ego in viā <u>plaustrum</u> nōn videō.	_____	_____
4. Sunt multa <u>flūmina</u> in Ītaliā.	_____	_____
5. Longum <u>carmen</u> dē flūminibus poēta scrībit.	_____	_____
6. Sunt multa <u>oppida</u> in Ītaliā.	_____	_____
7. <u>Iter</u> ad haec oppida est perīculōsum.	_____	_____
8. Igitur tuum <u>cōnsilium</u> est bonum.	_____	_____
9. Nunc <u>onera</u> servī ad raedam portant.	_____	_____
10. <u>Tempus</u> est discēdere.	_____	_____

PRACTICE THREE

Place the correct Nominative or Accusative ending on the noun stem to complete the meaning of the sentence. Then translate each sentence into English.

1. Meum cubicul_____ in villā est parvum.

   _____

2. In villā est magnum gaudi_____ quod pater ab urbe redit.

   _____

3. Ex carrō oner_____ servī capiunt.

   _____

4. Nōm_____ illī puerō est Lūcius.

   _____

5. Is carmin_____ cantāre amat.

   _____

6. Lūcius mūner_____ vidēre etiam amat.

   _____

7. Lītōr_____ sunt pulchra.

   _____

8. Mānē per lītus est silenti _____.

   _____

9. Dīc mihi nōm_____ canis quī in Tartarō habitat.

   _____

10. Canis Cerberus tria capit_____ sed modo ūnum corp_____ habet.

    _____

11. Ego mīra mūner_____ spectāre volō.

    _____

12. Ego scelestōs virōs prope amphitheātrum videō. Convocāte auxili_____
    celeriter!_____

    _____

PRACTICE FOUR

Translate the following into English and then answer the questions under each sentence:

1. Corpus lupus trahit._____

   How can you decide whether **corpus** or **lupus** is the subject of the sentence?_____

   _____

2. Magister ad forum iter facit._____

   How can you decide whether **magister** or **iter** is the subject of the sentence?_____

   _____

3. Multa plaustra in viā puellae nōn vident._____

   How can you decide whether **plaustra** or **puellae** is the subject of the

   sentence?_____

   _____

4. Claudia mūnera spectāre nōn amat._____

   How can you decide whether **Claudia** or **mūnera** is the subject of the

   sentence?_____

   _____

PRACTICE FIVE

Read the following story. Circle all Nominative forms and underline all Accusative forms. Then answer in English the questions found below.

Familia Claudiae

Claudia est puella Rōmāna quae in villā magnā habitat. Familia Claudiae est magna. Ea mātrem, patrem, duōs frātrēs, et ūnam sorōrem habet. Eius avus quī senātor est etiam in villā cum Claudiā habitat. Avus multōs servōs habet. Aliī in agrīs labōrant et multum frūmentum parant, aliī magna onera in plaustrīs pōnunt. Pater Claudiae est poēta. Eī nōmen Claudius est. Is in villā sedet et multa carmina scrībit. Claudia et soror nōn sunt discipulae in lūdō. Māter puellās domī docet. Duo frātrēs sunt discipulī. Mox cum magistrō frātrēs ad lītus iter facient.

soror, sorōris, f.	*sister*	**frūmentum, -ī,** n.	*grain*
avus, -ī, m.	*grandfather*	**lūdus, -ī,** m.	*school*
aliī. . . aliī	*some . . . others*	**domī**	*at home*

1. Where does Claudia live?_____

2. What family members live with Claudia?_____

   _____

3. What do the slaves place in the wagons?_____

4. What does her father write?_____

5. Who teaches the girls?_____

6. Soon where will her brothers go?_____

CHAPTER III — THE GENITIVE CASE

CASE	1st Declen. (f.)	2nd Declen. (m.)	3rd Declen. (m.)
SING.			
Nom.	fābula	hortus	senātor
Gen.	fābul**ae**	hort**ī**	senatōr**is**
Acc.	fābulam	hortum	senatōrem
PL.			
Nom.	fābulae	hortī	senatōrēs
Gen.	fābul**ārum**	hort**ōrum**	senatōr**um**
Acc.	fābulās	hortōs	senatōrēs

CASE	1st Declen. (m.)	2nd Declen. (n.)	3rd Declen. (n.)
SING.			
Nom.	agricola	baculum	nōmen
Gen.	agricol**ae**	bacul**ī**	nōmin**is**
Acc.	agricolam	baculum	nōmen
PL.			
Nom.	agricolae	bacula	nōmina
Gen.	agricol**ārum**	bacul**ōrum**	nōmin**um**
Acc.	agricolās	bacula	nōmina

IDENTIFICATION OF NOUN DECLENSIONS

In Latin, **the Genitive Singular Case ending** is used to identify the declension to which a noun belongs. Just as people have a last name to identify the family to which they belong, so do nouns. When you look up a Latin noun in the dictionary, you will find the following arrangement:

amīca, -ae, f.	*friend*	**īnsula, -ae,** f.	*apartment*
servus, -ī, m.	*slave*	**puer, -ī,** m.	*boy*
perīculum, -ī, n.	*danger*	**līberī, -ōrum,** m.	*children*
mīles, mīlitis, m.	*soldier*	**corpus, corpōris,** n.	*body*

NOTA BENE:
   The Genitive Singular ending of all first declension nouns is **-ae**.
   The Genitive Singular ending of all second declension nouns is **-ī**.
   The Genitive Singular ending of all third declension nouns is **-is**.
   The base or stem of any Latin noun is the Genitive Singular form minus the Genitive ending. Certain nouns that occur only in plural form such as **līberī, -ōrum** will be listed in the dictionary with a Genitive Plural ending of **-ārum, -ōrum, -um,** or **-ium**.

PRACTICE ONE

Circle the Genitive ending of each noun. Then identify the noun declension as 1st, 2nd, or 3rd.

_____1. onus, oneris   _____5. pīctūra, pīctūrae   _____9. servus, servī

_____2. mīles, mīlitis   _____6. oppidum, oppidī   ____10. raeda, raedae

_____3. pater, patris   _____7. līberī, līberōrum   ____11. flūmen, flūminis

_____4. puella, puellae   _____8. arbor, arboris   ____12. vir, virī

PRACTICE TWO

Using the Latin to English dictionary at the back of this book, write out the correct Genitive form for each of the following nouns. Then identify the declension of each noun. The first one is done for you.

<u>2nd</u> 1. rāmus, rām   <u>rāmī</u>   _____11. tempus, tempōr _____

_____2. canis, can   _____   _____12. lupus, lup   _____

_____3. casa, cas   _____   _____13. lēx, lēg   _____

_____4. aurīga, aurīg   _____   _____14. vōx, vōc   _____

_____5. nūntius, nūnti _____   _____15. fīlia, fīli   _____

_____6. raeda, raed   _____   _____16. mūnus, mūner _____

_____7. rēx, rēg   _____   _____17. īra, īr   _____

_____8. fābula, fābul _____   _____18. gaudium, gaudi _____

_____9. verbum, verb _____   _____19. frāter, frātr   _____

____10. īnsula, īnsul _____   _____20. incola, incol   _____

PRACTICE THREE

Draw a circle around the stem of each noun. Then write the Genitive Plural form of each noun in the blank.

1. cubiculī _____   5. mātris _____   9. nepōtis _____

2. capitis _____   6. oneris _____   10. populī _____

3. pīrātae _____   7. cistae _____   11. rēgis _____

4. vīlicī _____   8. silvae _____   12. mīlitis _____

PRACTICE FOUR

On a separate sheet of paper, complete noun declension charts for the following nouns. Use the noun declension chart on page thirteen as your guide.

1. auxilium, -ī   3. coquus, -ī   5. arbor, arboris

2. familia, -ae   4. lītus, litōris   6. puer, puerī

HOW THE GENITIVE CASE IS USED IN LATIN

1) The genitive of **possession** expresses the answer to the question, "Whose is it?"

Baculum **vīlicī** est magnum.   *The **overseer's** stick is large.*

or

*The stick **of the overseer** is large.*

2) **"Of Phrases"** At times the English preposition **of** is used to express a relationship between two nouns or a noun and an adjective that does not express ownership or possession.

Magnus numerus **servōrum** in agrīs labōrat.
*A great number **of slaves** is working in the fields.*

Hortus est plēnus **flōrum**.   *The garden is full **of flowers**.*

Key words which will often be followed by a Genitive Case noun are:

cōpia, -ae, f.	*supply (of)*	**cupidus, -a, -um**	*desirous (of)*
numerus, -ī, m.	*number (of)*	**plēnus, -a, -um**	*full (of)*
pars, partis, f.	*part (of)*		

NOTA BENE:
Remember that there is no word for the English preposition **of** in Latin.

PRACTICE FIVE

Look at each picture. Then copy each pair of words changing either the first or second word of the pair into the Genitive Case to describe the picture. Finally, translate your resulting phrase into English. The first one is done for you.

1. speculum   fēmina
    speculum fēminae
    the mirror of the woman

4. rīpa   rīvus
    _____
    _____

2. senatōrēs togae
    _____
    _____

5. mīlitēs gladiī
    _____
    _____

3. canis   capita
    _____
    _____

6. carmina poēta
    _____
    _____

7. <u>domina   īra</u>

8. <u>crīnēs   puella</u>

9. <u>statua   prīnceps</u>

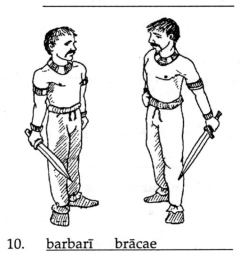

10. <u>barbarī   brācae</u>

PRACTICE SIX

*In each of the following sentences, circle the noun that would be in the Genitive Case in Latin. Then mark whether the Genitive Case noun shows **possession** or is in a **phrase**.*

	Possession	Phrase
1. Antonius' sister is Antonia.	_____	_____
2. A number of her friends is in the house.	_____	_____
3. They are very desirous of her many dresses.	_____	_____
4. A number of soldiers is working.	_____	_____
5. They are preparing a supply of grain for the winter.	_____	_____
6. The weapons of the soldiers are lying nearby.	_____	_____
7. The streets are full of noise this morning.	_____	_____
8. I can hear the peddlers' shouts.	_____	_____
9. Now I can see the bread vendor's cart.	_____	_____

PRACTICE SEVEN

In each sentence, circle all nouns that are in the Genitive Case. Then translate the sentence into English.

1. Vīlicus īram dominī timet._____

   _____

2. Vīlicus omnēs servōs et ancillās in āream villae vocat._____

   _____

3. Ille nūntium dominī legit._____

   _____

4. Numerus servōrum mandāta dominī nōn amat._____

   _____

5. Servī mandāta aut vīlicī aut dominī facere nōn volunt._____

   _____

6. Ancillae dominae in culīnā labōrant._____

   _____

7. Labor ancillārum in culīnā est difficilis._____

   _____

8. Nunc pars cēnae est parāta._____

_____

9. Numerus ancillārum in cubiculīs labōrat._____

_____

10. Ancillae vestēs parēntum in cistās pōnunt._____

_____

11. Dum ancillae labōrant, nūtrīx in peristȳliō villae sedet et īnfantem
dominae spectat._____

_____

_____

PRACTICE EIGHT

Using the pool of names and the information below, fill in the missing members of the family tree on page twenty-one.

Iūlia Māior	Iūlia Minor	Marcella Minor
Marcella Māior	Antōnia Māior	Antōnius
Livia	C. Octavius	C. Marcellus

Familia Augustī

1. Augustus erat frāter Octaviae et nepōs Balbī.

2. Iūlia Māior erat soror Iūliī Caesaris et uxor Balbī.

3. Octavia erat fīlia C. Octaviī et Atiae.

4. Iūlius Caesar erat avunculus Atiae.

5. Octavia duōs marītōs C. Marcellum et Antōnium habēbat.

6. Octavia et C. Marcellus erant parēntēs Marcellae Māioris et Marcellae Minoris.

7. Pater Antōniae Māioris et Antōniae Minoris erat Antōnius.

8. Parēntēs Augustī erant C. Octavius et Atia.

9. Augustus duās uxōrēs Scriboniam et Liviam habēbat.

10. Māter Iūliae Minoris erat Scribonia.

11. Iūlia Minor erat uxor M. Marcellī quī erat cōnsōbrīnus Iūliae Minoris.

12. M. Marcellus erat fīlius C. Marcellī et nepōs C. Octaviī.

13. Avia Octaviae erat Iūlia Māior.

14. C. Octavius erat avus M. Marcellī.

15. Duae sorōrēs M. Marcellī erant Marcella Māior et Marcella Minor.

Family Tree Chart

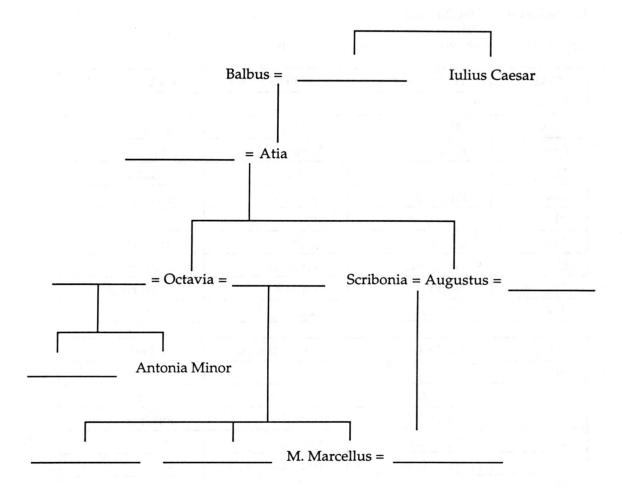

Balbus = _____ Iulius Caesar

_____ = Atia

_____ = Octavia = _____ Scribonia = Augustus = _____

Antonia Minor

_____

_____ _____ M. Marcellus = _____

CHAPTER IV — THE DATIVE CASE

. . . .

FORMATION OF THE DATIVE CASE

The chart below shows the endings for the Dative Case.

CASE	1st Declen. (f.)	2nd Declen. (m.)	3rd Declen. (m.)
SING.			
Nom.	fābula	hortus	senātor
Gen.	fābulae	hortī	senatōris
Dat.	fābul**ae**	hort**ō**	senatōr**ī**
Acc.	fābulam	hortum	senatōrem
PL.			
Nom.	fābulae	hortī	senatōrēs
Gen.	fābulārum	hortōrum	senatōrum
Dat.	fābul**īs**	hort**īs**	senatōr**ibus**
Acc.	fābulās	hortōs	senatōrēs

CASE	1st Declen. (m.)	2nd Declen. (n.)	3rd Declen. (n.)
SING.			
Nom.	agricola	baculum	nōmen
Gen.	agricolae	baculī	nōminis
Dat.	agricolae	baculō	nōminī
Acc.	agricolam	baculum	nōmen
PL.			
Nom.	agricolae	bacula	nōmina
Gen.	agricolārum	baculōrum	nōminum
Dat.	agricolīs	baculīs	nōmin**ibus**
Acc.	agricolās	bacula	nōmina

NOTA BENE:
All nouns of the first declension have Dative endings of **-ae** and **-īs.**
All nouns of the second declension have Dative endings of **-ō** and **-īs.**
All nouns of the third declension have Dative endings of **-ī** and **-ibus.**

PRACTICE ONE

On a separate sheet of paper, complete noun declension charts for the following nouns.
Use the noun declension chart on page twenty-one as your guide.

1. culīna, -ae, f.
2. lupus, -ī, m.
3. īnfāns, īnfantis, m./f.
4. aurīga, -ae, m.
5. mandātum, -ī, n.
6. iter, itineris, n.

HOW THE DATIVE CASE IS USED

1) Indirect Object - In a sentence, the person or animal (never an inanimate object) to whom one gives, shows, or tells something takes the Dative Case. In Latin there is no preposition which precedes the indirect object. In English, you may have the preposition "to" preceding the indirect object.

Senātor epistulam **tabellāriō** dat.   *The senator gives the courier the letter.*

or

The senator gives the letter to the courier.

Certain verbs of giving, showing, and telling can take an indirect object. The following "Dative verbs" often include an indirect object in the sentence:

dēmōnstrō, -āre, -āvī, -ātus	*to point out (to)*
dīcō, dīcere, dīxī, dictus	*to tell (to)*
do, dāre, dedī, dātus	*to give (to)*
dōnō, -āre, -āvī, -ātus	*to give (to)*
inquit	*he, she says (to)*
mandō, -āre, -āvī, ātus	*to entrust (to)*
mōnstrō, -āre, -āvī, -ātus	*to show (to)*
nārrō, āre, -āvī, -ātus	*to tell (to)*
respondeō, respondere, respondī, responsus	*to respond (to)*
trādō, trādere, trādidī, trāditus	*to hand over (to)*

2) Special Verbs - The Dative Case is also found with these four special verbs:

appropīnquo, -āre, āvī, -ātus	*to approach*
licet, licēre, licuit	*to allow, to permit*
necesse esse	*to be necessary*
occurrō, occurrere, occurrī, occursus	*to meet, to run into*

Senātor et fīliī **Forō** appropīnquant.   *The senator and his sons approach the Forum.*
Mox **aliīs senātōribus** occurrent.   *Soon they will meet the other senators.*
Nōn licet **puerīs** in Cūriam īre.   *It is not allowed for the boys to enter the Senate House.*

Manēre extrā Cūriam **puerīs** necesse est.   *It is necessary for the boys to remain outside the senate house.*

NOTA BENE:
   For sentences using the verbs **licet** and **necesse esse**, the English translation of the word in the Dative Case will often employ the English preposition "for".

PRACTICE TWO

Look at what each picture describes. Circle the correct Latin form to complete the sentence. Then translate the Latin sentence into English.

1. Bēstiārius (leōnem/ leōnī) _____

   videt. _____
   _____
   _____

2. Bēstiārius (leōnem/ leōnī) _____

   appropīnquat. _____
   _____
   _____

3. Puer (quaestiōnem/quaestiōnī)

   magistrī audit. _____
   _____
   _____

4. Puer (magistrō/magistrum) _____

   respōnsum dat. _____
   _____
   _____

5. In popīnā mīles (amīcōs/ amīcīs) occurrit.

_____

_____

_____

6. Mīles (amīcīs/amīcōs) salūtat.

_____

_____

_____

PRACTICE THREE
Read the following story and underline all verbs which can take a Dative construction.

A Very Special Apple

Paedagōgus fābulam līberīs semper nārrāre amat. Hodiē, eīs fābulam dē tribus deābus nārrat.

Quaeque dea mīrissimum malum habēre voluit. In hōc malō verbum "Pulcherrimae" scrīptum est. Iūdex certāminis erat Paris, fīlius Trōiānī rēgis. Brevī tempōre quaeque dea dōnum ferens Paridī appropīnquāvit.

Minerva Paridī vītam plēnam fāmae dāre voluit. Iūnō eī sapientiam et potestātem magnī rēgis dāre voluit. Venus Paridī pulcherrimam fēminam dāre voluit.

Paris Venerī appropīnquāvit et eī malum dedit. Eius dōnum erat optimum.

5

quisque, quaeque, quidque	_each_	**Minerva, -ae,** f.	_The goddess Minerva_
mīrissimus, -a, -um	_very wonderful_	**Iūnō, Iūnōnis,** f.	_The goddess Juno_
mālum, -ī, n.	_apple_		
Pulcherrimae	_"To the Fairest"_	**sapientia, -ae,** f.	_wisdom_
iūdex, iūdicis, m.	_judge_	**potestās, potestātis,** f.	_power, authority_
certāmen, certāminis, n.	_contest_	**Venus, Veneris,** f.	_The goddess Venus_
Paris, Paridis, m.	_Paris, a Trojan prince_	**optimus, -a, -um**	_best_
dōnum ferens	_bringing a gift_		

PRACTICE FOUR

From the story "A Very Special Apple" find the following:

Four Indirect Objects

1._____

2._____

3._____

4._____

Two Dative Nouns with
Special Verbs

1._____

2._____

PRACTICE FIVE

Identify whether the word in bold face is Dative or Accusative. Then translate each sentence into English.

	Dative	Accusative
1. Dominus mandāta **vīlicō** dat.	_____	_____
2. **Servō** exīre in urbem licet.	_____	_____
3. Ille **tabernīs** in urbe appropīnquat.	_____	_____
4. Servus novam **tunicam** ēmere vult.	_____	_____
5. Mercātor multās **tunicās** servō mōnstrat.	_____	_____
6. **Mercatōrī** pecūniam dat.	_____	_____
7. Mercātor novam tunicam **servō** trādit.	_____	_____
8. Deinde servus **amīcō** occurrit.	_____	_____

	Dative	Accusative
9. Servus et amīcus **iter** ad popīnam faciunt.	_____	_____

_____

| 10. In popīnā amīcus servō **fābulam** nārrat. | _____ | _____ |

_____

PRACTICE SIX
Place the correct Dative or Accusative endings in the blanks to complete the sentences.

Aeneas and His Men Arrive at Carthage

Nāvēs Aenēae et sociōrum litōr_____ prope Carthāginem appropīnquant. Mox
Aenēae et soci_____ īre in urbem licet. Virī multa nova aedifici_____Carthāginis
vident. Virī rēgīn_____ Dīdōnī occurrunt. Ea pulchram urb_____ eīs
mōnstrat. Servī rēgīnae cēn_____ parant. Rēgīna Dīdō fābul_____ dē
itineribus Aenēae audīre vult. Igitur Aenēas Dīdōn_____ longam fābulam   5
dē itineribus suīs nārrat.

| **Aenēās, -ae**, m. | *Aeneas* | **Dīdō, Dīdōnis**, f. | *Dido, Queen of Carthage* |

PRACTICE SEVEN
Based on the story above, answer the following questions <u>in complete Latin sentences</u>.

1. Where are Aeneas and his men allowed to go?_____

_____

2. Whom do they meet?_____

_____

3. Who prepares the dinner?_____

_____

4. What does the hostess request of Aeneas?_____

_____

CHAPTER V — MORE ACCUSATIVE CASE

. . . .

REVIEW OF ACCUSATIVE CASE ENDINGS

Below is the chart highlighting the Accusative endings for the declensions of nouns we have reviewed so far.

CASE	1st Declen. (f.)	2nd Declen. (m.)	3rd Declen. (m.)
SING.			
Nom.	fābula	hortus	senātor
Gen.	fābulae	hortī	senatōris
Dat.	fābulae	hortō	senatōrī
Acc.	fābul**am**	hort**um**	senatō**rem**
PL.			
Nom.	fābulae	hortī	senatōrēs
Gen.	fābulārum	hortōrum	senatōrum
Dat.	fābulīs	hortīs	senatōribus
Acc.	fābul**ās**	hort**ōs**	senatō**rēs**

CASE	1st Declen. (m.)	2nd Declen. (n.)	3rd Declen. (n.)
SING.			
Nom.	agricola	baculum	nōmen
Gen.	agricolae	baculī	nōminis
Dat.	agricolae	baculō	nōminī
Acc.	agricol**am**	bacul**um**	nōmen
PL.			
Nom.	agricolae	bacula	nōmina
Gen.	agricolārum	baculōrum	nōminum
Dat.	agricolīs	baculīs	nōminibus
Acc.	agricol**ās**	bacul**a**	nōmin**a**

NOTA BENE:
> The Accusative Singular of all three declensions ends in -**m**, except for third declension neuter nouns.
> The Accusative Plural of all three declensions of masculine and feminine nouns ends in -**s**.
> The Nominative and Accusative Plural of third declension nouns is identical.
> The Nominative Singular form of a 2nd declension neuter noun ends in -**um**.
> The Nominative and Accusative forms of a neuter noun are always identical.
> For all three declensions the Nominative and Accusative neuter plural ending is -**a**.

PRACTICE ONE

On a separate sheet of paper, complete noun declension charts for the following nouns. Use the noun declension chart on page twenty eight as your guide.

1. cēna, -ae, f.
2. socius, -ī, m.
3. uxor, uxōris, f.
4. pīrāta, -ae, m.
5. verbum -ī, n.
6. lītus, litōris, n.

MORE USES OF THE ACCUSATIVE CASE

In Chapters I and II we reviewed the use of the Accusative Case to indicate the direct object in a sentence.

1) Direct Object - the person or object that receives the action of the verb.

Puella novam **stolam** gerit.	*The girl wears a new dress.*
Domina **ancillam** in culīnā invenit.	*The mistress finds the slave girl in the kitchen.*

The Accusative Case is also used in the following instances:

2) The objects of **certain prepositions** are in the Accusative Case. Many of these prepositons express motion towards.

ad + acc.	*to, towards*	**prope** + acc.	*near*
in + acc.	*into*	**trans** + acc.	*across*
per + acc.	*through*		

Ego **ad villam** ambulō.	*I walk to the farmhouse.*
Servī **per agrōs** ambulant.	*The slaves walk through the fields.*

NOTA BENE:
Do not confuse the direct object of a sentence with the object of a preposition. A direct object will **never** have a preposition in front of it. The object of a preposition **always** will have a preposition in front of it.

3) The Accusative Case is also used to express the length or **duration of time** of an event.

Servī **multās horās** in agrīs labōrant.	*The slaves work for many hours in the fields.*
Multōs diēs per Viam Appiam iter faciēbāmus.	*For many days, we traveled along the Appian Way.*

NOTA BENE:
Duration of time always involves a time expression like day, month, year, hour, etc. It answers the question **For how long.** In English look for the key word **for** followed by a time word. Remember in Latin, duration of time never uses a preposition for the word **for.**

Below are some words commonly used in time expressions.

annus, -ī, m.	*year*	**mēnsis, mēnsis**, m.	*month*
diēs, -eī, m.	*day*	**tempus, tempōris**, n.	*time*
hōra, -ae, f.	*hour*		

PRACTICE TWO

Read through the paragraph and list below each noun and pronoun in the Accusative Case and its use: a. direct object, b. object of a preposition, or c. duration of time.

Antonia's Morning

Multās horās Antōnia librum legens in villā sēderat. Cotīdiē, librōs legere sōlēbat. Nunc in hortum īre et pulchrōs flōrēs spectāre voluit. Prīmō, puellae trans atrium in tablīnum ambulāre necesse erat. Paulisper Antōnia capsam in tablīnō petēbat. Puella in pavīmentō prope mēnsam patris eam invēnit. Nunc ē tablīnō per ātrium et in hortum ambulāre poterat.   5

legens	reading		flōs, flōris, m.	flower
sōlebat	she was accustomed		capsa, -ae, f.	a case for books
			mēnsa, -ae, f.	desk

	Acc. Case	Use		Acc. Case	Use
1.	_____	_____	7.	_____	_____
2.	_____	_____	8.	_____	_____
3.	_____	_____	9.	_____	_____
4.	_____	_____	10.	_____	_____
5.	_____	_____	11.	_____	_____
6.	_____	_____	12.	_____	_____

PRACTICE THREE

Select the correct translation to complete the underlined phrase. Place the letter of your answer in the space provided.

_____1. The girls walk <u>into the farmhouse</u> to say good-bye.

    a. in villā   b. in villam   c. villam

_____2. Antonia asks her friend to write <u>many letters</u>.

    a. multae epistulae   b. multās epistulās   c. multīs epistulīs

_____3. The slaves are walking <u>through the house</u> with Antonia's trunks.

    a. per villam   b. trans villam   c. prope villam

_____4. The slaves walk <u>towards the carriage</u> with the trunks.

    a. carrum   b. per carrum   c. ad carrum

_____5. They place <u>the trunks</u> in the wagon.

    a. cistam   b. cistae   c. cistās

_____6. Other slaves are standing <u>near the wagon</u>.

    a. ad carrum   b. prope carrum   c. in carrum

_____7. After Antonia left, her friend was sad <u>for many days</u>.

    a. multōs diēs   b. multī diēs   c. multīs diebus

PRACTICE FOUR

Select the word or phrase which best completes the sentence. Place the letter of your answer in the blank provided. Then translate the sentence into English.

_____1. Multī servī_____ nōn amant.   a. vīlicī   b. vīlicō   c. vīlicum

_____

_____2. Nōn iam est lūx, sed vīlicus servīs_____ dat.

                  a. mandāta   b. mandātī   c. mandātō

_____

_____3. Servī ad_____ ambulant.   a. agrī   b. agrōs   c. agrīs

_____

_____4. Aliī servī prope _____ labōrant.   a. villam   b. villae   c. villā

_____

_____5. Iter ad_____ est longum.   a. urbis   b. urbs   c. urbem

_____

_____6. Parēntēs et līberī in carrō _____ iter faciunt.

                  a. multae hōrae   c. multās hōrās
                  b. multārum hōrārum

_____

_____7. Diū familia iter per_____ facit.

                  a. Viam Appiam   c. Viā Appiā
                  b. Viae Appiae

_____

_____8. Familia prope_____ urbis avō occurrit.

                  a. portae   b. portā   c. portam

_____

PRACTICE FIVE

Using the pool of words below, fill in the missing blanks in the story. Each word may be used only once.

A Visit to the Forum

Hodiē _____ duōs fīliōs ad forum ducit. Ubi in _____
        1   2

ambulant, puerī multa _____ cōnspiciunt. In forō sunt multī
                                     3

_____. Mercatōrēs cibum, _____, et vestēs populō vendunt.
     4   5

Magister _____ docet. _____ fābulam magistrō recitant. Nunc
                    6   7

pater et _____ Cūriae appropīnquant. Prope _____ complurēs
          8   9

senatōrēs stant. Ūnus ex senatōribus _____ puerōrum salūtat.
                                    10

_____ pater senatōrī dīcit. Pater puerōrum in Cūriam
          11

it. Quod puerīs Cūriam intrāre nōn licet, paedagōgus domum _____
                                                          12

dūcit.

Cūriam	fīliī	patrem
forum	brevī tempore	puerōs
discipulī	pater	discipulōs
mercatōrem	Cūria	fīliōs
librōs	breve tempus	liber
spectāculum	mercatōrēs	spectācula

CHAPTER VI — THE ABLATIVE CASE

. . . .

FORMATION OF THE ABLATIVE CASE

The chart below shows the endings for the Ablative Case.

CASE	1st Declen. (f.)	2nd Declen. (m.)	3rd Declen. (m.)
SING.			
Nom.	fābula	hortus	senātor
Gen.	fābulae	hortī	senatōris
Dat.	fābulae	hortō	senatōrī
Acc.	fābulam	hortum	senatōrem
Abl.	fābulā	hortō	senatōre
PL.			
Nom.	fābulae	hortī	senatōrēs
Gen.	fābulārum	hortōrum	senatōrum
Dat.	fābulīs	hortīs	senatōribus
Acc.	fābulās	hortōs	senatōrēs
Abl.	fābulīs	hortīs	senatōribus

CASE	1st Declen. (m.)	2nd Declen. (n.)	3rd Declen. (n.)
SING.			
Nom.	agricola	baculum	nōmen
Gen.	agricolae	baculī	nōminis
Dat.	agricolae	baculō	nōminī
Acc.	agricolam	baculum	nōmen
Abl.	agricolā	baculō	nōmine
PL.			
Nom.	agricolae	bacula	nōmina
Gen.	agricolārum	baculōrum	nōminum
Dat.	agricolīs	baculīs	nōminibus
Acc.	agricolās	bacula	nōmina
Abl.	agricolīs	baculīs	nōminibus

NOTA BENE:
  The Dative and Ablative Plural of each declension are the same.
  You can distinguish whether a word is in the Dative or Ablative Case by its use in a sentence.

PRACTICE ONE

On a separate sheet of paper, complete noun declension charts for the following nouns.
Use the noun declension chart on page thirty-three as your guide.

    1. rēgīna, -ae, f.   3. marītus, -ī, m.   5. arbor, arboris, f.

    2. incola, -ae, m.   4. dōnum, -ī, n.   6. carmen, carminis, n.

USES OF THE ABLATIVE CASE

There are a number of uses for the Ablative Case. Many but <u>not all</u> uses of the Ablative Case can be translated into English with the English words **by, with** or **from.**

USES OF THE ABLATIVE THAT REQUIRE A PREPOSITION IN LATIN

1) Place Where - This use involves the Latin preposition **in** to show location.
    Pōnite cistās **in raedā.**   *Place the trunks **in the wagon.***

2) Special Prepositions - The objects of **certain prepositions** are in the Ablative Case. Many of these prepositions express location or motion away.

ā, ab + abl.	*away from*	**sine** + abl.	*without*
dē + abl.	*about, down from*	**sub** + abl.	*under*
ē, ex + abl.	*out of*		

    Puella **sub arbōre** sedet.   *The girl sits **under the tree.***
    Puer **ē villā** ambulat.   *The boy walks **out of the farmhouse.***

3) Accompaniment - This use involves the person or animal **with whom** you do the action. In Latin, you always use the preposition **cum.**
    Cum patre ad villam ambulāmus.   *We walk to the farmhouse **with father.***

4) Agent - This use involves the person or animal who does the action in a sentence that contains a verb in the passive voice. In Latin, you always use the preposition **ā, ab.**
    Servī **ā vīlicō** vocantur.   *The slaves are summoned **by the overseer.***

USES OF THE ABLATIVE THAT DO NOT REQUIRE A PREPOSITION IN LATIN

5) Means - This use involves **the concrete object** or **thing** with which you complete the action of the verb.
    Epistulam **stilō** scrībō.   *I write the letter **with the pen.***

6) Manner - This use involves **the abstract object** with which you complete the action of the verb.
    Mīlitēs **māximā virtūte** pugnant.   *The soldiers fight **with the greatest courage.***

7) Time When - The Ablative Case is also used to express the **actual time** of an event.
    Ūnā horā discēdimus.   *We leave **in one hour.***
    Tribus diēbus ad Graeciam nāvigābimus.   ***Within three days** we will sail to Greece.*

HINTS ON HOW TO IDENTIFY THE VARIOUS USES OF THE ABLATIVE CASE

1) The Ablatives of **Means, Manner,** and **Accompaniment** can all involve a **"with" phrase** in their English translation. To be able to tell them apart, remember the following:

> **Accompaniment** - Takes the Latin prepositon **cum** followed by a noun indicating a person or animal.

> **Means** - No preposition in Latin. The noun or pronoun in the Ablative Case is always a tangible object never a person or animal.

> **Manner** - No preposition in Latin. The noun or pronoun in the Ablative Case is always an abstract noun like joy, happiness, swiftness, etc.

2) Time When always involves a time expression like day, month, year, hour, winter, evening, etc. It answers the question **When.** In English, look for the key words **in, on, at,** or **within** followed by a time word. Remember in Latin, Time When never uses a preposition for the English meaning **in, on, at,** or **within.**

PRACTICE TWO

Draw a picture that illustrates each of the following sentences. Then name the kind of ablative phrase used in the sentence.

1. Uxor cum marītō in tablīnō sedet.

2. Magnō studiō puellae lānam trahunt. (lānam trahere, *to spin wool*)

3. Nauta ā pīrātīs capitur.

4. Prīmā lūce servī ē villā in agrōs eunt.

5. Dēfessī servī sub arboribus sedent.

6. Īrātus magister discipulum baculō verberat.

PRACTICE THREE

Read through the story below. Answer in Latin the questions below concerning the story "A Trip to the Baths."

A Trip to the Baths

Antōnius et amīcī cum paedagōgō ad thermās ambulant. In thermīs nōn modo sunt piscīnae, palaestrae, et stadia sed etiam hortī, bibliothēcae (Graecae et Latīnae), et scholae ubi poētae magnō studiō novissima carmina recitant. Cubicula thermārum multīs pīctūris ōrnantur. Cotīdiē thermae sunt plēnae hominum.

Prīmō Antōnius in palaestrā lūdit et in stadiō currit. Deinde in frīgidarium it. Ē   5
frīgidariō ad tepidarium et caldarium it. Nunc puer est dēfessus. In hortō thermārum sub arbore sedet et librum legit.

paedagōgus, -ī, m.	*tutor*	**schola, -ae, f.**	*hall*
thermae, -ārum, f.	*baths*	**frīgidarium, -ī, n.**	*cold pool*
stadium, -ī, n.	*running track*	**tepidarium, -ī, n.**	*warm pool*
bibliothēca, -ae, f.	*library*	**caldarium, -ī, n.**	*hot pool*
palaestra, -ae, f.	*place of exercise*		

1. With whom does Antonius go to the baths?_____

2. What type of libraries are found at the baths?_____

3. How do the poets recite their poems?_____

4. When are the baths crowded?_____

5. Where does Antonius sit and read his book?_____

PRACTICE FOUR

From the story above find an example of each use of the Ablative Case listed below. Write your answer in the space provided.

1. Abl. of Place Where_____

2. Abl. of Time_____

3. Abl. with Special Preposition_____

4. Abl. of Means_____

5. Abl. of Manner_____

6. Abl. of Accompaniment_____

PRACTICE FIVE

Select the correct translation of the underlined word and place the letter of your answer in the space provided.

_____1. In a few months, Antonius' grandfather will arrive in Rome.

    a. Paucōrum mēnsium   b. Paucīs mēnsibus   c. Paucōs mēnsēs

_____2. Antonius' grandfather will travel with his wife.

    a. uxōrī   b. uxōre   c. cum uxōre

_____3. He will travel to Brundisium from Athens by ship.

    a. nāvibus   b. ā nāve   c. nāve

_____4. Antonius has not yet heard the news about his grandfather.

    a. dē avō   b. avōs   c. ex avō

_____5. The slave wishing to run away walks out of the farmhouse towards the woods.

    a. ē villā   b. in villam   c. dē villā

_____6. The overseer and other slaves with dogs chase him through the woods.

    a. canibus   b. canēs   c. cum canibus

_____7. The runaway slave tries to hide himself in a ditch.

    a. in fossam   b. fossae   c. in fossā

_____8. In a short time the dogs find him.

    a. Brevī tempōre   b. Brevī tempōrī   c. Breve tempus

_____9. The runaway slave is beaten by the master.

    a. ē dominō   b. ā dominō   c. cum dominō

___ 10. The master beats him with a stick.

    a. baculō   b. cum baculō   c. dē baculō

PRACTICE SIX

Select the correct Latin phrase which best completes the meaning of the sentence. Place the letter of your answer in the space provided. Then translate the sentence into English.

_____1. _____puellae ē lectīs surgunt.

    a. Prīmā lūce   b. Ad prīmam lūcem   c. Prīma lūx

_____

_____2. _____ientaculum edunt.

    a. In culīnā   b. Ē culīnā   c. Dē culīnā

_____

_____3. _____ ad silvam currunt.

    a. Ē villā   b. In villam   c. Sub villā

_____4. Quod diēs est calidus, _____ puellae sedent.

    a. ab arboribus   b. sub arboribus   c. in arborēs

_____5. _____ puellae carmina cantant.

    a. Amīcārum   b. Amīcās   c. Cum amīcīs

PRACTICE SEVEN

Read the story below. Then list all nouns or noun-adjective combinations in the Ablative Case that are found in the story. Finally, identify each use of the Ablative. The first one is done for you.

Time for Dinner

    Antōnius cum amīcō in culīnam ambulat. Coquus iūs magnō cocleare miscet. Magnō studiō coquus cēnam familiae parat. Sorōrem in ātriō sedentem Antōnius videt. Ea sine magnō studiō lānam trahit. Māter ē cubiculō in trīclīnium ambulat. Brevī tempōre, pater ā Cūriā domum pervenit. Omnēs in trīclīniō iam sunt. Cibus ā servīs fertur. Servī fercula cībī ad mēnsam ferunt. Familia digitīs et etiam pāne cēnam edit. In mēnsā, 5 Rōmanī cocleara nōn pōnunt. Dum edunt, pater eīs novissimās fābulās dē prīncipe nārrat.

iūs, iūris, n.	_soup_	**digitus, -ī,** m.	_finger_
cocleare, coclearis, n.	_ladle, spoon_	**pānis, pānis** m.	_bread_
lānam trahere	_to spin wool_	**novissimus, -a, -um**	_most recent_
ferculum, -ī, n.	_serving tray_		

        Examples of Ablatives   **Use of Ablative**

1. _____cum amīcō_____   _abl. of accompaniment_

2. _____   _____

3. _____   _____

4. _____   _____

5. _____   _____

(cont.)

6. _____   _____

7. _____   _____

8. _____   _____

9. _____   _____

10. _____   _____

11. _____   _____

12. _____   _____

13. _____   _____

14. _____   _____

CHAPTER VII — THE VOCATIVE CASE

· ·

FORMATION OF THE VOCATIVE CASE

In most instances, the Vocative Case forms are identical to their corresponding Nominative Case forms. Only second declension masculine singular nouns ending in **-us** or **-ius** have a different ending for the Vocative Case. Look at the chart below:

CASE	1st Declen. (m.)	1st Declen. (f.)	2nd Declen. (m.)
SING.			
Nom.	agricola	puella	vir
Voc.	agricola	puella	vir
PL.			
Nom.	agricolae	puellae	virī
Voc.	agricolae	puellae	virī

CASE	2nd Declen. (m.)	2nd Declen. (m.)	3rd Declen. (m.)
SING.			
Nom.	servus	fīlius	senātor
Voc.	serve	fīlī	senātor
PL.			
Nom.	servī	fīliī	senatōrēs
Voc.	servī	fīliī	senatōrēs

NOTA BENE:
    The Vocative Singular of 2nd declension nouns ending in **-us** is **-e**.
    The Vocative Singular of 2nd declension nouns ending in **-ius** is **-ī**.

PRACTICE ONE

Give the corresponding Vocative form for each of the following nouns.

1. rēgīna _____
2. Antōnius _____
3. Cornēliī _____
4. pater _____
5. iūdicēs _____
6. Claudius _____
7. Claudia _____
8. līberī _____
9. fīliī _____
10. Augustus _____

11. hostēs _____
12. Brūtus _____
13. Cornēlius _____
14. puer _____
15. marītī _____
16. Mārcus _____
17. Claudiī _____
18. senatōrēs _____
19. Antōnia _____
20. fīlius _____

HOW THE VOCATIVE CASE IS USED

The Vocative Case is used for nouns of direct address. Direct address means that one person is saying something **to another person**, not something **about the person**.

Voc:	**Serve**, cistam ad raedam portā!	*Slave, carry the trunk to the wagon.*
Nom:	**Servus** cistam ad raedam portat.	*The slave carries the trunk to the wagon.*
Voc:	**Puellae**, cūr in villā cantātis?	*Girls, why are you singing in the house?*
Nom:	**Puellae** in villā cantant.	*The girls are singing in the house.*

NOTA BENE:
   A noun in the Vocative Case is set off by commas from the rest of the sentence.
   A noun in the Vocative Case is usually found with a verb in the second person or in the imperative mood.

PRACTICE TWO

Match the correct English and Latin translations for the following sentences. Place the letter of your answer in the space provided.

____1. Canēs, nōlite lātrāre.

____2. Labōrāte celeriter, servī.

____3. Coquus cībum parat.

____4. Redī domum, Antōnia.

____5. Flāviī iter Brundisium faciunt.

____6. Antōnia domum redit.

____7. Cībum parā, coque.

____8. Claudī, magistrō respondē.

a. The cook prepares the food.

b. The Flavians travel to Brundisium.

c. Work quickly, slaves.

d. Dogs, don't bark.

e. Cook, prepare the food.

f. The dogs do not bark.

g. Claudius, respond to your teacher.

h. Flavius, travel to Brundisium.

i. Antonia returns home.

j. Claudius responds to his teacher.

k. Return home, Antonia.

l. The slaves work quickly.

PRACTICE THREE

Provide the information requested for the underlined phrase in each sentence. The first one is done for you.

	Nom. or Voc.	Sing. or Plural	Latin Form
1. <u>Antonius</u>, come here!	<u>Voc.</u>	<u>S</u>	<u>Antōnī</u>
2. <u>Antonius</u> arrives at the forum.	____	____	_____
3. The <u>boys</u> are running.	____	____	_____
4. Why are you running, <u>boys</u>?	____	____	_____
5. <u>Cook</u>, prepare the food immediately.	____	____	_____
6. The <u>cook</u> quickly prepares the food.	____	____	_____
7. <u>Claudius</u> writes me a letter.	____	____	_____
8. <u>Claudius</u>, please write me a letter.	____	____	_____
9. Leave the forum now, <u>senators</u>!	____	____	_____
10. Why are the <u>senators</u> now leaving the forum?	____	____	_____

PRACTICE FOUR

Using the pool of names below, complete the following paragraph. A name may be used more than once.

The Day Julius Caesar Died

_____ est bonus amīcus Iūliī Caesaris. Aliī virī Brūtō dīcunt,

<u>   </u>1

" Nōnne, _____, Iūlius Caesar rēx esse vult? Rōmānī rēgēs nōn amant.

      2

Necesse est nōbīs Iūlium Caesarem necāre. _____, nōbīscum venī!"

      3

_____ diū cōgitat. Deinde Brūtus dīcit, "_____ est

     4   5

meus amīcus sed rēgēs nōn amō. Ego vōbīscum ībō."

Nunc _____ ad Senātum īre parat. Uxor Calpurnia eī dīcit,

     6

" Nōlī īre, _____. Ego aliquid malī tibi timeō. Manē domī!"

     7

_____ uxōrī dīcit, " _____, nōlī timēre. _____

     8   9   10

sunt fortūnātī. Mihi nūllum malum accidet."

Iūlius Caesar Brūtum et aliōs prope Senātum videt. _____ et aliī clamant,

     11

"Salve, _____." _____ virīs appropīnquat. Nunc virōs in

     12   13

mānibus gladiōs tenentēs videt. Aliī virī cum Brūtō gladiīs Iūlium Caesarem

pellunt. Ūltima verba quae Iūlius Caesar dīcit sunt, " Et tū, _____!"

     14

Brūtus	Iūlius Caesar	Iūliī
Brūte	Iūlī Caesar	Calpurnia

CHAPTER VIII — PREPOSITIONS

. . . .

CASES FOR OBJECTS OF PREPOSITIONS

The prepositions we have reviewed so far have taken either the Accusative or Ablative Cases. Here is a summary of those prepositions and a few new prepositions as well.

Prepositions whose objects are in the Accusative Case:

ad + acc.	*to, towards*	**prope** + acc.	*near*
in + acc.	*into*	**super** + acc.	*over, above*
per + acc.	*through*	**trans** + acc.	*across*

Prepositions whose objects are in the Ablative Case:

ā, ab + abl.	*away from, by*	**in** + abl.	*in, on*
cum + abl.	*with*	**prō** + abl.	*for, in front of,*
dē + abl.	*about, down from*		*on behalf of*
ē, ex + abl.	*out of*	**sine** + abl.	*without*
		sub + abl.	*under*

NOTA BENE:
   Prepositions that take the Accusative Case show *motion towards.*
   Many prepositions which take the Ablative Case show *location, motion away,* or *separation.*
   Be careful of the Latin preposition **in.** Followed by the Accusative it means **into;** followed by the Ablative it means **in** or **on.**
   The following mnemonic aid can help you remember which prepositions take the Ablative Case.
   <u>S</u>ub, <u>I</u>n, <u>D</u>e, <u>S</u>ine, <u>P</u>ro, <u>A</u>b, <u>C</u>um, <u>E</u>x: S I D S P A C E, the "ABLATIVE Astronaut"

PRACTICE ONE

Place an X by the correct response for each picture.

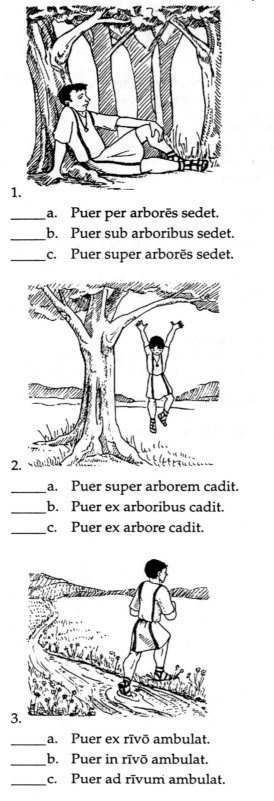

1.

_____ a. Puer per arborēs sedet.

_____ b. Puer sub arboribus sedet.

_____ c. Puer super arborēs sedet.

2.

_____ a. Puer super arborem cadit.

_____ b. Puer ex arboribus cadit.

_____ c. Puer ex arbore cadit.

3.

_____ a. Puer ex rīvō ambulat.

_____ b. Puer in rīvō ambulat.

_____ c. Puer ad rīvum ambulat.

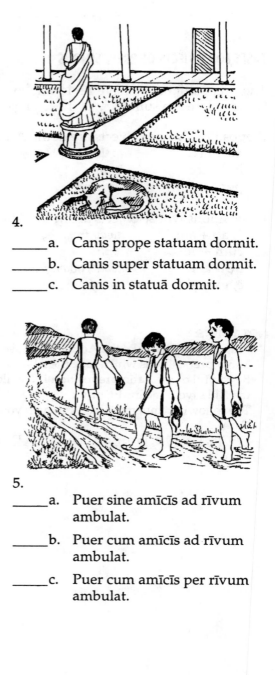

4.

_____ a. Canis prope statuam dormit.

_____ b. Canis super statuam dormit.

_____ c. Canis in statuā dormit.

5.

_____ a. Puer sine amīcīs ad rīvum ambulat.

_____ b. Puer cum amīcīs ad rīvum ambulat.

_____ c. Puer cum amīcīs per rīvum ambulat.

PRACTICE TWO

For each of the sentences below underline the prepositional phrase. Then list whether the Acc. or Abl. Case is being used for the object of the preposition. Next translate the prepositonal phrase into English. The first one is done for you.

		Case	Translation
1.	Antōnius <u>in culīnam</u> ambulat.	Acc.	into the kitchen
2.	Ille ā coquīs salūtatur.		
3.	Ille in culīnā cum coquō et aliīs servīs stat.		
4.	Coquus in furnō pīnguissimum porcum habet.		
5.	Pater ad Cūriam it.		
6.	Sine fīliīs discēdit.		
7.	Prope forum aliīs senatōribus occurrit.		
8.	Senatōrēs eī novissimās fābulās dē bellō dīcunt.		
9.	Quod dies est frīgidus, mīlitēs trans flūmen natāre nōlunt.		
10.	Prō glōriā fāmāque mīlitēs pugnant.		
11.	Claudia lānam trahens in hortō sedet.		
12.	Illa ex hortō ambulat.		
13.	Nunc in silvam ambulāre vult.		
14.	Super silvam avēs volant.		

pīnguissimus, -a, -um   *very fat*   **avis, avis, m./f.**   *bird*

PRACTICE THREE

Match the Latin prepositional phrase with its English meaning. Place the letter of your answer in the space provided. You will not use every answer.

____1. per silvam   a. in the houses

____2. cum servīs   b. away from the forum

____3. prope forum   c. by the slaves

____4. prō pecūniā   d. through the woods

____5. in villīs   e. without money

____6. ad forum   f. near the forum

____7. sine pecūniā   g. for money

____8. ē villīs   h. with the slaves

____9. ā forō   i. into the house

___10. sub arbōribus   j. about the slaves

___11. ab servīs   k. out of the houses

___12. in villam   l. over the trees

                                  m. under the trees

                                  n. to the forum

PRACTICE FOUR

Make each sentence say the opposite. Then translate the new sentence into English. The first one is done for you.

1. Tū in hortum curris. _____ Tū ex hortō curris. _____

   _____ You are running out of the garden. _____

2. Avēs sub arboribus volant. _____

   _____

3. Puellae prope piscīnam stant. _____

   _____

4. Pater ē tablīnō cum servō ambulat. _____

   _____

5. Familia iter ad urbem facit._____

_____

6. Ē cistā vestēs nōn sunt._____

_____

vestimenta virorum

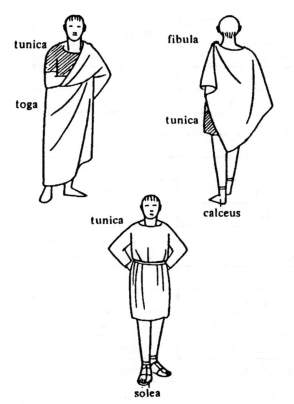

tunica

toga

fibula

tunica

calceus

tunica

solea

vestimenta mulierum

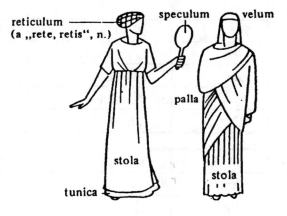

reticulum
(a „rete, retis", n.)

speculum

velum

palla

stola

stola

tunica

CHAPTER IX — REVIEW OF ALL CASES AND THEIR USES

....

REVIEW OF CASE ENDINGS

The following charts summarize the case endings for declensions I–III which we have reviewed in the previous chapters.

CASE	1st Declen. (f.)	2nd Declen. (m.)	3rd Declen. (m.)
SING.			
Nom.	fābula	hortus	senātor
Gen.	fābulae	hortī	senatōris
Dat.	fābulae	hortō	senatōrī
Acc.	fābulam	hortum	senatōrem
Abl.	fābulā	hortō	senatōre
PL.			
Nom.	fābulae	hortī	senatōrēs
Gen.	fābulārum	hortōrum	senatōrum
Dat.	fābulīs	hortīs	senatōribus
Acc.	fābulās	hortōs	senatōrēs
Abl.	fābulīs	hortīs	senatōribus

CASE	1st Declen. (m.)	2nd Declen. (n.)	3rd Declen. (n.)
SING.			
Nom.	agricola	baculum	nōmen
Gen.	agricolae	baculī	nōminis
Dat.	agricolae	baculō	nōminī
Acc.	agricolam	baculum	nōmen
Abl.	agricolā	baculō	nōmine
PL.			
Nom.	agricolae	bacula	nōmina
Gen.	agricolārum	baculōrum	nōminum
Dat.	agricolīs	baculīs	nōminibus
Acc.	agricolās	bacula	nōmina
Abl.	agricolīs	baculīs	nōminibus

PRACTICE ONE

On a separate sheet of paper decline the following nouns. Use the chart on page fifty as your guide.

1. pīrāta, -ae, m.
2. mandātum, -ī, n.
3. tempus, tempōris, n.
4. mīles, mīlitis, m.
5. nūntius, -ī, m.
6. servus, -ī, m.

PRACTICE TWO

On a separate sheet of paper give the Vocative Singular and Plural forms for numbers 1, 4, 5, and 6, from Practice One.

PRACTICE THREE

Change each of the following underlined singular nouns to its correct plural form as determined by the context of the sentence. Make any other changes in the sentence as necessary. Then translate the new sentence into English.

1. Puella sub <u>arbore</u> sedet.

2. Puella <u>amīcam</u> videt.

3. Amīca ad <u>arborem</u> ambulat.

4. <u>Nūntius</u> villae appropīnquat.

5. Nūntius <u>epistulam</u> fert.

6. Pater epistulam <u>fīliō</u> mōnstrat.

7. <u>Puellae</u> ad forum īre nōn licet.

8. Puellae cum <u>ancillā</u> ad tabernam eunt.

9. Puellae in lectīcīs <u>iter</u> faciunt.

PRACTICE FOUR

Change each of the following underlined plural nouns to its correct singular form. Make any other changes in the sentence as necessary. Then translate the new sentence into English.

1. Pater ad Cūriam sine <u>servīs</u> it._____

_____

2. In Cūriā aliīs <u>senatōribus</u> dīcit._____

_____

3. Multum dē <u>bellīs</u> in Britanniā audit._____

_____

4. <u>Vīlicī</u> sunt īrātī quod servī nōn labōrant._____

_____

5. Vīlicus servōs īgnāvōs <u>baculīs</u> verberat._____

_____

6. <u>Mātrēs</u> līberōs petunt._____

_____

7. Māter <u>puerōs puellāsque</u> in hortō invenit._____

_____

8. Vir solus prope <u>magna aedificia</u> ambulat._____

_____

9. Praedōnēs <u>hominibus</u> appropīnquant._____

_____

10. <u>Praedōnēs</u> hominem pellunt._____

_____

11. Vir gravia <u>vulnera</u> accipit._____

_____

12. Statim, <u>servī</u>, ferte mihi auxilium!_____

_____

REVIEW OF CASE USES

Below is a summary of the cases and their uses that we have reviewed so far.

I. NOMINATIVE CASE

    A. As Subject

        Puella in agrīs ambulat.
        *The **girl** walks in the fields.*

    B. As Predicate

        Antōnia est **mea amīca.**
        *Antonia is **my friend.***

II. GENITIVE CASE

    A. To Show Possession

        Baculum **vīlicī** est magnum.
        *The **overseer's** stick is large.*

    B. "Of Phrases"

        Hortus est plēnus **flōrum.**
        *The garden is full **of flowers.***

III. DATIVE CASE

    A. As Indirect Object

        Senātor epistulam **tabellariō** dat.
        *The senator gives the letter **to the messenger.***

    B. With Special Verbs
       (*appropīnquāre, licēre,*
       necesse est, occurrere)

        Senātor et fīliī **forō** appropīnquant.
        *The senator and his sons approach **the forum.***

IV. ACCUSATIVE CASE

    A. As Direct Object

        Puella **novam stolam** gerit.
        *The girl wears a **new dress.***

    B. Objects of Certain Prepositions

        Servī **per agrōs** ambulant.
        *The slaves walk **through the fields.***

    C. Duration of Time

        Servī **multās horās** in agrīs labōrābant.
        *The slaves were working **for many hours** in the fields.*

V. ABLATIVE CASE

    A. Place Where

        Pōnite cistās **in raedā!**
        *Place the trunks **in the wagon.***

    B. Objects of Certain Prepositions

        Puella **sub arbōre** sedet.
        *The girl sits **under the tree.***

    C. Accompaniment

        Cum patre ad forum ambulābimus.
        ***With father** we will walk to the forum.*

    D. Agent

        Servī **ā vīlicō** vocantur.
        *The slaves are called **by the overseer.***

    E. Means

        Epistulam **stilō** scrībō.
        *I write the letter **with a pen.***

    F. Manner

        Mīlitēs **maximā virtūte** pugnant.
        *The soldiers fight **with the greatest courage.***

    G. Time When

        Unā horā discēdēmus.
        ***In one hour** we will leave.*

VI. VOCATIVE CASE

    A. For Nouns in Direct Address

        Serve, cistās ad raedam portā!
        ***Slave,** carry the trunks to the wagon!*

PRACTICE FIVE

Identify the case and use of the underlined word(s), then select the correct translation of the underlined word(s). The first one is done for you.

	Case	**Use**

<u>a</u> 1. Father made a journey <u>by ship</u> to Athens.   <u>Abl.</u>   <u>Means</u>

    a. nāve   b. nāvis   c. ā nāve   d. nāvem

_____2. He made the journey <u>without his family</u>.   _____   _____

    a. cum familiā   b. familiīs   c. sine familiā   d. familiā

_____3. On the way, his ship was attacked <u>by pirates</u>.   _____   _____

    a. pīrātās   b. ā pīrātīs   c. dē pīrātīs   d. ā pīrātā

_____4. Antonia is sitting <u>in the garden</u>.   _____   _____

    a. in hortum   b. ex hortō   c. super hortum   d. in hortō

_____5. Soon her mother walks <u>into the garden</u>.   _____   _____

    a. in hortum   b. ex hortō   c. ad hortum   d. in hortō

_____6. Her mother tells Antonia <u>about father's trip</u>.   _____   _____

    a. dē itineris patre b. dē itinere patris c. patrem itineris d. iter patris

_____7. Where are the <u>boys</u>?   _____   _____

    a. puerōs   b. puerī   c. puerīs   d. puer

_____8. <u>With their tutor</u> the boys walk to school   _____   _____

    a. Prō paedagōgō b. Cum paedagōgō c. Paedagogīs d. Paedagogum

_____9. <u>In a short time</u>, they arrive at school   _____   _____

    a. Brevī tempōre b. Brevis tempōris c. Breve tempus d. Brevī tempōrī

___ 10. The boys recite a poem <u>to their teacher</u>.   _____   _____

    a. magistrum   b. magistrō   c. ad magistrum   d. magistrī

___ 11. Then they write their lessons <u>with a stilus</u>.   _____   _____

    a. cum stilō   b. stilō   c. stilum   d. prō stilō

___ 12. Mother <u>in a loud voice</u> is shouting at the cook.   _____   _____

    a. magnā vōce   b. magnam vōcem c. magna vōx   d. magnae vōcis

___ 13. The cook approaches <u>mother</u>.   _____   _____

    a. mātrem   b. mātre   c. mātrī   d. ad mātrem

___ 14. "<u>Cook</u>, prepare dinner now!" says mother.   _____   _____

    a. Coquus   b. Coquō   c. Coque   d. Coquī

		Case	Use

___ 15. The cook hastily returns <u>to the kitchen</u>. _____ _____

    a. trans culīnam   b. prope culīnam   c. in culīnā   d. ad culīnam

___ 16. The cook begins to hum <u>a song</u>. _____ _____

    a. carmina   b. carminis   c. carminī   d. carmen

___ 17. <u>Mother</u> is very annoyed by his humming. _____ _____

    a. Māter   b. Mātrēs   c. Mātrī   d. Mātrem

___ 18. The forum is full <u>of soldiers</u> today. _____ _____

    a. mīlitis   b. mīlitī   c. mīlitēs   d. mīlitum

___ 19. In the forum a merchant shows new tunics to <u>a soldier</u>. _____ _____

    a. mīlitem   b. mīlitī   c. mīlitibus   d. mīles

___ 20. The soldier buys several new <u>tunics</u>. _____ _____

    a. tunicās   b. tunicīs   c. tunicae   d. tunicam

PRACTICE SIX

Select the correct answer to complete the meaning of each sentence. Place the letter of your answer in the space provided.

____1. Pater fābulam_____ nārrābat.

    a. puerōs   b. puerī   c. puer   d. puerīs

____2. _____Antōnius per agrōs currit.

    a. Magnā celeritāte   c. Magna celeritās
    b. Magnam celeritātem   d. Magnārum celeritātum

____3. Herī multa_____ legī.

    a. carmen   b. carminum   c. carmina   d. carminibus

____4. Pater_____ est vir praeclārissimus.

    a. Antōnium   b. Antōniō   c. Antōniī   d. Antōnius

____5. Ubi sunt_____?

    a. equus   b. equī   c. equōs   d. equīs

____6. Canem_____ nōlīte verberāre!

    a. baculum   b. baculō   c. baculī   d. baculōrum

____7. Dux_____ iter Rōmam nōn faciet.

    a. mīlitibus   b. mīles   c. mīlitēs   d. cum mīlitibus

(cont.)

_____ 8. Hodiē villa nōn est plēna_____ .

    a. servī   b. servōs   c. servōrum   d. servīs

_____ 9. _____ domī manēre nōn vult.

    a. Puellae   b. Puella   c. Puellis   d. Puellā

___ 10. _____, servōs ex agrīs vocā!

    a. Vīlice   b. Vīlicus   c. Vīlicī   d. Vīlicō

___ 11. Ancilla celeriter cībum_____ posuit.

    a. super mēnsam   b. per mēnsam   c. dē mensā   d. in mensā

___ 12. Nōn licet_____ sine paedagōgō in urbem īre.

    a. līberīs   b. līberum   c. līberōs   d. līberī

___ 13. Canis_____ dormit ubi sōl nōn lūcet.

    a. in carrum   b. sub carrō   c. super carrum   d. dē carrō

___ 14. _____ pater ē prōvinciā domum reveniet.

    a. Duōbus mēnsibus   c. Duōs mēnsēs

    b. Duōrum mēnsium   d. Duo mēnsēs

___ 15. _____ est magnum flūmen.

    a. Trans villam   b. In villā   c. Super villam   d. Prope villam

___ 16. Meus amīcus_____ captus est.

    a. pīrātīs   b. pīrātae   c. ā pīrātīs   d. pīrātās

___ 17. _____ meum amīcum invenīre nōn poterāmus.

    a. Multōs diēs   c. Multōrum diērum

    b. Multīs diēbus   d. Multī diēs

___ 18. Nautae dē nāve _____ vidēre possunt.

    a. litōrum   b. lītus   c. litōribus   d. litōrī

___ 19. In litōre nautae_____ occurrunt.

    a. uxōrem   b. uxōre   c. uxōris   d. uxōribus

___ 20. Servī in hortō_____ nōn labōrābant.

    a. magnīs studiīs   c. magnō studiō

    b. magnum studium   d. magna studia

CHAPTER X — FOURTH AND FIFTH DECLENSION NOUNS

. . . .

FORMATION OF FOURTH AND FIFTH DECLENSION NOUNS

In this chapter we will review the forms of Fourth and Fifth Declension nouns. Look at the chart below:

CASE	1st (f.)	2nd (m)	3rd (m.)	4th (m.)	5th (f.)
SING.					
Nom.	puella	servus	homō	lātrātus	spēs
Gen.	puellae	servī	hominis	lātrātūs	speī
Dat.	puellae	servō	hominī	lātrātuī	speī
Acc.	puellam	servum	hominem	lātrātum	spem
Abl.	puellā	servō	homine	lātrātū	spē
PL.					
Nom.	puellae	servī	hominēs	lātrātūs	spēs
Gen.	puellārum	servōrum	hominum	lātrātuum	spērum
Dat.	puellīs	servīs	hominibus	lātrātibus	spēbus
Acc.	puellās	servōs	hominēs	lātrātūs	spēs
Abl.	puellīs	servīs	hominibus	lātrātibus	spēbus

NOTA BENE:
Fourth Declension is often called the "u" declension because of the number of u's used in the endings. Most nouns of the fourth declension are masculine.
Fifth Declension is often called the "e" declension because of the number of e's used in the endings. Most nouns of the fifth declension are feminine.
The Vocative endings of fourth and fifth declension nouns are identical to the Nominative endings.

Below are listed some common nouns of the fourth and fifth declensions.

Fourth Declension

aestus, -ūs, m.	*heat*	**rīsus, -ūs,** m.	*laughter, smile*
arcus, -ūs, m.	*arch*	**sonitus, -ūs,** m.	*sound*
domus, -ūs, f.	*home*	**strepitus, -ūs,** m.	*noise, clattering*
frūctus, -ūs, m.	*fruit*	**tumultus, -ūs,** m.	*commotion*
lātrātus, -ūs, m.	*barking*	**ūsus, -ūs,** m.	*use, advantage*
manus, -ūs, f.	*hand, band of men*		

Fifth Declension

diēs, -eī, m.	*day*	rēs, reī f.	*thing, matter*
faciēs, -ēī, f.	*appearance, face*	speciēs, -ēī f.	*sight, kind*
fidēs, -ēī, f.	*pledge, trust*	spēs, -eī, f.	*hope*

PRACTICE ONE

On a separate sheet of paper, complete noun declension charts for the following nouns.
Use the noun declension chart on page fifty-seven as your guide.

1. arcus, -ūs, m.

2. manus, -ūs, f.

3. rēs, reī, f.

4. fidēs, -ēī, f.

PRACTICE TWO

Circle the Genitive ending of each noun. Then identify the noun declension as 1st, 2nd, 3rd., 4th, or 5th.

_____1. cista, cistae

_____2. uxor, uxōris

_____3. faciēs, faciēī

_____4. auxilium, auxiliī

_____5. corpus, corpōris

_____6. lātrātus, lātrātūs

_____7. urbs, urbis

_____8. līberī, līberōrum

_____9. frūctus, frūctūs

_____10. homō, hominis

_____11. spēs, speī

_____12. hortus, hortī

PRACTICE THREE

Using the Latin to English dictionary at the back of this book, write out the correct Genitive form for each of the following nouns. Then identify the declension of each noun. The first one is done for you.

<u>3rd</u>_1. mīles, mīlit <u>mīlitis</u>

_____2. arcus, arc _____

_____3. fīlius, fīli _____

_____4. pīrāta, pīrāt _____

_____5. nōmen, nōmin_____

_____6. puella, puell _____

_____7. rēs, r _____

_____8. verbum, verb _____

_____9. vōx, vōc _____

_____10. manus, man _____

_____11. pater, patr _____

_____12. corpus, corpōr _____

_____13. ūsus, ūs _____

_____14. vir, vir _____

_____15. custōs, custōd _____

_____16. baculum, bacul _____

_____17. diēs, di _____

_____18. marītus, marīt _____

_____19. nepōs, nepōt _____

_____20. speciēs, speci _____

PRACTICE FOUR

Change each of the following underlined singular nouns to its correct plural form as determined by the context of the sentence. Make any other changes in the sentence as necessary. Then translate the new sentence into English.

1. Magnum <u>sonitum</u> in viā audiō._____

   _____

   _____

2. <u>Faciēs</u> ancillae est misera._____

   _____

   _____

3. Ille <u>manū</u> equōs nōn verberāvit._____

   _____

   _____

4. In prōvinciā est perīculōsa <u>rēs</u>. _____

   _____

   _____

5. Mox <u>arcuī</u> in forō appropīnquābimus._____

   _____

   _____

PRACTICE FIVE

Change each of the following underlined plural nouns to its correct singular form as determined by the context of the sentence. Make any other changes in the sentence as necessary. Then translate the new sentence into English.

1. <u>Frūctūs</u> in hīs arboribus sunt optimī._____

   _____

   _____

2. Duōbus <u>diēbus</u> pater domum perveniet._____

   _____

   _____

3. Domina <u>rīsūs</u> in <u>faciēbus</u> servōrum nōn amat._____

   _____

   _____

4. Carmen dē <u>rēbus</u> nātūrīs ā poētā Lucretiō scrīptum est. _____

   _____

   _____

5. <u>Speciēbus</u> mortuōrum gladiatōrum in arēnā permoveor._____

   _____

   _____

6. Puer <u>tumultibus</u> <u>strepitibusque</u> canum ē somnō excitābitur. _____

   _____

   _____

....

Pronouns

INTRODUCTION — TYPES OF PRONOUNS

Pronouns are words that take the place of nouns. In this section of the workbook, you will review the following types of pronouns.

1. Personal	**ego**	*I*
	tū	*you*
2. Demonstrative	**is, ea, id**	*he, she, it*
	hic, haec, hoc	*this (one)*
	ille, illa, illud	*that (one)*
3. Relative	**quī, quae, quod**	*who, which, that*

NOTA BENE:
    The demonstrative pronouns are also used as adjectives:
hic vir, *this man*; **illa fēmina**, *that woman*.

CHAPTER I — PERSONAL PRONOUNS AND *IS, EA, ID*

. . . .

The personal pronouns of the first person are **ego**, *I*, and **nōs**, *we*; of the second person, **tū**, *you*, and **vōs**, *you*. There are no personal pronouns for *he, she, it, they*; often the demonstrative **is, ea, id** is used. These pronouns are declined as follows:

	First Person	**Second Person**	**Third Person**		
SING.			*m.*	*f.*	*n.*
Nom.	ego	tū	is	ea	id
Gen.	meī	tuī	eius	eius	eius
Dat.	mihi	tibi	eī	eī	eī
Acc.	mē	tē	eum	eam	id
Abl.	mē	tē	eō	eā	eō
PL.					
Nom.	nōs	vōs	eī	eae	ea
Gen.	nostrum	vestrum	eōrum	eārum	eōrum
Dat.	nōbīs	vōbīs	eīs	eīs	eīs
Acc.	nōs	vōs	eōs	eās	ea
Abl.	nōbīs	vōbīs	eīs	eīs	eīs

NOTA BENE:
   In the plural, the pronoun **is, ea, id** has the letter **e** as a stem to which the endings of **magnus, magna, magnum** are added.
   The Genitive plural endings (as always) end in the letters **-um**.
   The Dative and Ablative plural forms are (as always) the same.
   The preposition **cum** is connected to **mē, tē, nōbīs**, and **vōbīs**, e.g., **mēcum, tēcum**.

PRACTICE ONE
Circle the pronoun(s) in each sentence and then translate the sentence into English.

1. Puella mēcum ambulat. _____

2. Eī eam vidēbant. _____

3. Ea eōs vidēbat. _____

4. Īte nōbīscum! _____

5. Tē in villā nōn inveniō. _____

6. Nārrā eīs fābulam. _____

7. Is vōbīscum ībit. _____

8. Ea nōbīscum ībit. _____

9. Eī cum eā ībunt. _____

10. Pecūniam vōbīs dabunt. _____

11. Eōrum equī sunt fortēs. _____

12. Eius pater est senātor. _____

13. Vōs nōn amāmus. _____

14. Vōs estis meī amīcī. _____

15. Parāte id nunc! _____

16. Audīvistīne eius ōrātiōnem? _____

17. Cēlā eōs in villā! _____

18. Dā eī sīgnum! _____

19. Eōrum librōs habuī. _____

20. Fer mihi auxilium! _____

21. Ferte nōbīs auxilium! _____

22. Eum eamque vidēbō. _____

23. Ubī tē petēmus? _____

24. Patrem eārum vīdimus. _____

25. Fer eam mihi! _____

26. Ego eum timeō. _____

27. Ego ea timeō. _____

28. Tēcum venient. _____

29. Ea eōs in forō invenit. _____

30. Tū nōs spectābās. _____

PRACTICE TWO

*Give the case, number, and Latin form (using **ego, tu,** and **is**) needed for the following underlined English pronouns and nouns. The first one is done for you.*

	Case	Number	Form		Case	Number	Form
1. Tell <u>it</u> <u>to me</u>!	acc.	s.	id	/	dat.	s.	mihi
2. <u>Claudia</u> is <u>their</u> friend.	___	___	___	/	___	___	___
3. <u>They</u> are <u>her</u> friends.	___	___	___	/	___	___	___
4. <u>We</u> gave <u>her</u> a new stola.	___	___	___	/	___	___	___
5. I went <u>with them</u>.	___	___	___	/	___	___	___
6. It scared <u>me</u>.	___	___	___	/	___	___	___
7. <u>We</u> will leave <u>with her</u>.	___	___	___	/	___	___	___
8. <u>You</u> are <u>his</u> worst enemies.	___	pl.	___	/	___	___	___
9. <u>His</u> slaves do not like <u>you</u>.	___	___	___	/	___	s.	___
10. <u>They</u> do not like <u>her</u>.	___	___	___	/	___	___	___
11. Put <u>them</u> <u>in that wagon</u>.	___	___	___	/	___	___	___
12. <u>Those things</u> scared <u>you</u>.	___	___	___	/	___	pl.	___
13. <u>I</u> will approach <u>it</u> carefully.	___	___	___	/	___	___	___
14. Will <u>he</u> go <u>with us</u>?	___	___	___	/	___	___	___
15. Will <u>you</u> take <u>her</u> there?	___	s.	___	/	___	___	___
16. <u>Those boys</u> saw <u>us</u>.	___	___	___	/	___	___	___
17. <u>It</u> is necessary for <u>him</u> to go.	___	___	___	/	___	___	___
18. <u>We</u> did not hear <u>you</u>.	___	___	___	/	___	s.	___
19. <u>He</u> hit <u>me</u> with the stick.	___	___	___	/	___	___	___
20. Lucius told <u>us</u> <u>those things</u>.	___	___	___	/	___	___	___
21. Take <u>me</u> <u>with you</u>!	___	___	___	/	___	pl.	___
22. Send <u>it</u> <u>to me</u>.	___	___	___	/	___	___	___
23. <u>I</u> will not laugh at <u>them</u>.	___	___	___	/	___	___	___
24. Where will <u>they</u> find <u>you</u>?	___	___	___	/	___	s.	___
25. Go <u>with me</u> to find <u>them</u>!	___	___	___	/	___	___	___

CHAPTER II — DEMONSTRATIVE PRONOUNS

. . . .

WHAT IS A DEMONSTRATIVE PRONOUN?

A demonstrative pronoun helps to indicate where an object is located in relationship to the speaker of the sentence. **Hic**, *this one* (pl. *these*) refers to an object that is close by. **Ille**, *that one* (pl. *those*) refers to an object that is in the distance.

Hic est amīcus prīncipis.	*This (man) is a friend of the emperor.* (i.e., someone near by)
Ille est amīcus prīncipis.	*That (man) is a friend of the emperor.* (i.e., someone in the distance)

FORMS

Below are the forms for **hic** and **ille**:

The Demonstrative Pronouns					
SING.	*m.*	*f.*	*n.*	*m.*	*f.*	*n.*
Nom.	hic	haec	hoc	ille	illa	illud
Gen.	huius	huius	huius	illius	illius	illius
Dat.	huic	huic	huic	illī	illī	illī
Acc.	hunc	hanc	hoc	illum	illa	illud
Abl.	hōc	hāc	hōc	illō	illā	illō
PL.						
Nom.	hī	hae	haec	illī	illae	illa
Gen.	hōrum	hārum	hōrum	illōrum	illārum	illōrum
Dat.	hīs	hīs	hīs	illīs	illīs	illīs
Acc.	hōs	hās	haec	illōs	illās	illa
Abl.	hīs	hīs	hīs	illīs	illīs	illīs

NOTA BENE:
   hic = *this one*; **hīc** = *here*. Always check to see if the **i** is long!

PRACTICE ONE

Circle the demonstrative pronoun(s) in each sentence and translate the sentence into English.

1. Ubī est māter hārum? _____

2. Illa dīcere nōn potes. _____

3. Hic est meus pater. _____

4. Dā illīs haec. _____

(cont.)

5. Illam nōn petīvimus. _____

6. Scrībīte nōmina hōrum. _____

7. Hae cum illīs ībunt. _____

8. Ille cum hīs ībit. _____

9. Mox hōs illōsque capiet. _____

10. Illās nōn amāmus. _____

11. Mātrem illius vīdī. _____

12. Dūc haec tēcum! _____

13. Dūc hanc tēcum! _____

14. Ille vēra hīs dīxit. _____

15. Huius crīnēs sunt pulchrī. _____

16. Illud mihi feret. _____

17. Tū huic fābulam nārrābis. _____

18. Amīcī illius sunt. _____

19. Ea hōc nōn invenit. _____

20. Cēlā hoc celeriter! _____

PRACTICE TWO

*Give the gender, number, case, and form of **hic** or **ille** needed for the following underlined English words or phrase. The first one is done for you.*

	Gender	Number	Case	Form
1. He approached <u>this man</u>.	m.	s.	dat.	huic
2. Beware <u>the dog.</u>				
3. He gave it <u>to those women</u>.				
4. Lucius lives <u>in this house</u>.				
5. Did you like <u>those things</u>.				
6. <u>That master</u> is very angry.				
7. We do not know <u>these women</u>.				
8. I am a friend <u>of that girl</u>.				
9. <u>That thing</u> always scares us.				
10. We gave orders <u>to that cook</u>.				
11. He will go <u>with this messenger</u>.				

	Gender	Number	Case	Form
12. Give the plans <u>to these girls</u>.	_____	_____	_____	_____
13. Show <u>those things</u> to me now!	_____	_____	_____	_____
14. Go <u>with these soldiers</u>!	_____	_____	_____	_____
15. We will send it <u>with that girl</u>.	_____	_____	_____	_____
16. <u>Those children</u> look tired.	_____	_____	_____	_____
17. I will finish <u>this thing</u> quickly.	_____	_____	_____	_____
18. The fate <u>of that woman</u> was sad.	_____	_____	_____	_____
19. My slave is <u>this man</u>.	_____	_____	_____	_____
20. Most of <u>those slaves</u> are thieves.	_____	_____	_____	_____

CHAPTER III — THE RELATIVE PRONOUN

FORMS AND USE OF THE RELATIVE PRONOUN

Below is the chart listing the forms of the relative pronoun:

The Relative Pronoun				
SING.	*m.*	*f.*	*n.*	English Translation
Nom.	quī	quae	quod	*who, which*
Gen.	cuius	cuius	cuius	*whose*
Dat.	cuī	cuī	cuī	*to whom, to which*
Acc.	quem	quam	quod	*whom, which*
Abl.	quō	quā	quō	*by, with, or from whom, which*
PL.				*or in which*
Nom.	quī	quae	quae	*who, which*
Gen.	quōrum	quārum	quōrum	*whose*
Dat.	quibus	quibus	quibus	*to whom, to which*
Acc.	quōs	quās	quae	*whom, which*
Abl.	quibus	quibus	quibus	*by, with, or from whom, which,*
				or in which

NOTA BENE:
   Who always translates the Nominative Case.
   Whose always translates the Genitive Case.
   Whom always translates a direct object (Acc.), an indirect object (Dat.) or an object of a preposition (Abl.).
   Who and *whom* refer to people and animals.
   Which refers to inanimate objects.
   The preposition **cum** is connected to Ablative forms, e.g., **quōcum, quibuscum.**

The relative pronoun is used to link or join a dependent clause to the main clause of the sentence. Look at the following sentences.

*Puerī, [***quōs*** *vīdistī], sunt meī amīcī.*   *The boys, [***whom*** *you saw], are my friends.*

*Urbs, [in ***quā*** *manēbāmus], erat magna.*   *The city, [in ***which*** *we stayed], was large.*

1) The **antecedent** is the noun or pronoun in the main clause that the relative pronoun refers to or replaces in the dependent clause. In the two sentences above, the antecedents are *Puerī* and *Urbs*.

2) The **gender** and **number** of the relative pronoun is determined by its antecedent. In the two sentences above, *puerī* is masculine plural, so **quōs** is masculine plural; *urbs* is feminine singular, so **quā** is feminine singular.

3) The **case** of the relative pronoun is determined by its use in the dependent clause. In the two sentences above, **quōs** is in the accusative case because it is the direct object of the verb, **vīdistī**, in the dependent clause; **quā** is in the ablative case because it is the object of the preposition, **in**, in the dependent clause.

NOTA BENE:
Relative clauses are often set off by commas from the rest of the sentence. Therefore punctuation can be a helpful cue in identifying a relative clause.

PRACTICE ONE

In the following English sentences, underline the relative pronouns and bracket the relative clauses. Draw an arrow (as in the examples on page sixty-eight) from the relative pronoun to its antecedent. Finally, list what case the relative pronoun would be in Latin. The first one is done for you.

Case in Latin

Nom. 1. The girl, [who is standing by the door], is my sister.

_____ 2. The girls, to whom I gave the money, were going to the circus.

_____ 3. We saw the boys whose teacher is well known to you.

_____ 4. The buildings, which he had seen, were in ruins.

_____ 5. The soldier did not like the others with whom he was traveling.

_____ 6. We watched the cook who was preparing our dinner.

_____ 7. The help, which the general needed, did not arrive in time.

_____ 8. The shop, in which I found my dress, was far away from my house.

_____ 9. He owned the horses with which the charioteer had won the race.

_____ 10. Antonia, whose mother you met, is the daughter of a senator.

PRACTICE TWO

In each of the following Latin sentences, underline the relative pronouns and bracket the relative clauses. Draw an arrow from the relative pronoun to its antecedent. Finally, translate the sentence into English. The first one is done for you.

1. Via, [quae nōn est lata], est plēna plaustōrum. <u>The road which is not wide is full of wagons.</u>

2. Haec est urbs, in quā multī cīvēs Rōmānī habitant. _____

3. Ego, quae sum tua amīca, tibi veritātem dīxī. _____

4. Pete servum cuius nōmen est Rufus. _____

5. Mīlitēs, quibus mandāta dedit, in caupōna sunt. _____

6. Ego puellās videō quae ad Forum ambulant. _____

7. Ille nūntiō dīxit quōcum iter faciēbās. _____

8. Pīrātae, reddīte pecūniam quam vōs cēpistis. _____

9. Ille ā virīs interfectus est quōrum sociī erant praedōnēs praeclārī. _____

10. In aedificiīs, quae incendiō vastāta erant, multī pauperēs habitābant. _____

11. Puerī, quōs ad Circum vīdistī, sunt fīliī senātōris. _____

_____

_____

12. Poēta, cuius librum legēbāmus, est cliēns senātōris. _____

_____

_____

13. Invēnērunt plaustrum quod in silvā cēlātum erat. _____

_____

_____

14. Pater nōbīs multās et mīrās fābulās, quae nōs omnēs delectābant, nārrāvit. _____

_____

_____

15. Plaustra, quae bovēs trāxērunt, erant gravia. _____

_____

_____

PRACTICE THREE

Select the correct Latin form of the relative pronoun for each of the following sentences.
Place the letter of your answer in the blanks provided.

_____1. Domūs, *which* sunt in Mōnte Palātīnō, māximae sunt.

   a. quam   b. quae   c. quās   d. quī

_____2. Ancillae, *to whom* mercātor vestīmenta vēndiderat, domum celeriter festīnāvērunt.

   a. quibus   b. quō   c. quās   d. quārum

_____3. Urbs, *which* visitāvērunt, erat pulchra.

   a. quod   b. quae   c. quam   d. quī

_____4. Ancillae, *who* in culīnā labōrant, semper sunt dēfessae.

   a. quī   b. cuius   c. quās   d. quae

_____5. Ā mercātōre, *whose* taberna sordida est, porcum nōn ēmēmus.

   a. cuī   b. quōrum   c. cuius   d. quō

_____6. Plaustrum, *which* mihi dedit, rotam frāctam habēbat.

   a. quō   b. quod   c. quae   d. quem

(cont).

_____7. Dux mandāta mīlitibus dedit *who* dīligenter audiēbant.

      a. quae   b. quōrum   c. quōs   d. quī

_____8. Parvae puellae, *whose* nūtrix est aegra, sunt miserae.

      a. quārum   b. quōrum   c. cuī   d. quās

_____9. Tuae sorōrēs, *with whom* iter faciēbam, mihi dē tē multās res nārrāvērunt.

      a. quācum   b. quās   c. quibuscum   d. quārum

___ 10. Servus, *whom* fīliī dominī saepe vexābant, erat īrātus.

      a. quī   b. quod   c. quōs   d. quem

PRACTICE FOUR

Rewrite each pair of sentences so that the second sentence becomes a dependent clause using a relative pronoun. Then translate the new sentence into English. The first one is done for you.

1. a. Ego puerum vīdī.
   b. Puerō librōs dōnāverās.

   <u>Ego puerum, cuī librōs dōnāverās, vīdī. I saw the boy to whom you had</u>

   <u>given the books.</u>

2. a. Antōnius et Lucius sunt bonī puerī.
   b. Paedagōgus puerōs ad lūdum dūcit.

3. a. Mea uxor est pulchra.
   b. Uxor longōs crīnēs habet.

4. a. Nūntius patrem vexābat.
   b. Verba nūntiī intellegere nōn poterat.

5. a. In lectīca erat infāns.
   b. Infantī ancilla aquam dedit.

_____

_____

_____

6. a. Dominus et amīcī lātrātum canum audiunt.
   b. Cum canibus fugitīvōs servōs petunt.

_____

_____

_____

CHAPTER IV — REVIEW OF ALL PRONOUNS

· ·

PRACTICE ONE

Identify the type of pronoun (personal, demonstrative, or relative) and case that would be used in Latin for each of the underlined English pronouns or nouns in the following sentences. The first one is done for you.

	Type of Pronoun	Case in Latin
1. <u>Their</u> horses always win the race.	Demon.	Gen.
2. <u>Those children</u> are well behaved.		
3. The battle, <u>which</u> was fought, took many Roman lives.		
4. <u>I</u> like to sing.		
5. Why did Lucius walk to school with <u>this boy</u>?		
6. The man, with <u>whom</u> you spoke, knows the emperor well.		
7. The paedagogus will go with <u>you</u> to the forum.		
8. The poet, <u>whose</u> poems are being recited, is not present.		
9. Did the slave give the message <u>to that man</u>?		
10. The slave women, <u>who</u> are working in the garden, are from Spain.		
11. The soldier told <u>us</u> an interesting story.		
12. The master has often punished <u>these slaves</u>.		

PRACTICE TWO

Circle the pronouns in each of the following sentences. Then translate each sentence into English.

1. Ea est intelligēns puella. _____

   _____

2. Meus pater, quī est praeclārus senātor, mox iter Rōmam faciet. _____

   _____

   _____

3. Statim mihi haec mōnstrā! _____

   _____

4. Servus, cuī dominus mandāta dedit, celeriter labōrem confēcit. _____

   _____

   _____

5. Ego cum amīcīs et tē ad Circum ībō. _____

   _____

6. Ubi tū illum in forō vīdistī? _____

   _____

7. Templa, quae prīnceps aedificāvērunt, multōs annōs manēbunt. _____

   _____

   _____

8. Dominus magnum praemium vōbīs dedit quod vōs fūrem invēnerātis. _____

   _____

   _____

9. Eius stola est pulchra. _____

   _____

10. Nōs haec dē prīncipe nōn audīverāmus. _____

    _____

11. Haec illōs, quī in viā stābant, diū spectābat. _____

    _____

12. Vōcēs illōrum, quī in culīnā clamābant, per tōtam villam audīrī poterant. _____

    _____

    _____

PRACTICE THREE

*Select the best answer from **a**, **b**, **c**, or **d**. Place the letter of your answer in the space provided.*

_____1. Templa, <u>which</u> in urbe vīdistī, erant māxima.

    a. quod   b. quam   c. quae   d. quārum

_____2. I received <u>her</u> letters yesterday.

    a. eam   b. eius   c. illārum   d. haec

_____3. Tell <u>me</u> the story about the brave boy.

    a. mē   b. illam   c. ego   d. mihi

_____4. Haec ad villam herī mīsit.

    a. He sent these things to the farm house yesterday.
    b. He sent these women to the farm house yesterday.
    c. He sent this thing to the farm house yesterday.
    d. He sent those men to the farm house yesterday.

_____5. Come <u>with us </u>to the games!

    a. nōbīscum   b. nōbīs   c. vōbīscum   d. nōs

_____6. Puellae ille fābulam longam nārrāvit.

    a. The girls told a long story to that boy.
    b. That boy told a long story to the girls.
    c. Those girls told a long story.
    d. That boy told a long story to the girl.

_____7. _____rēgem invenīre potueram.

    a. Nōs   b. Haec   c. Illī   d. Ego

_____8. Canēs fugītum, _____ nōmen est Rufus, nōn invēnērunt.

    a. illī   b. quī   c. cuius   d. quōrum

_____9. I did not know the girls <u>with whom</u> your daughter was walking.

    a. quibuscum   b. cum eīs   c. quās   d. quācum

___ 10. Mīles decem dēnāriōs <u>to those men</u> dedit.

    a. illōs   b. illīs   c. hīs   d. illum

___ 11. <u>You</u> all will ride with the coachman.

    a. Tū   b. Vōbīs   c. Tē   d. Vōs

___ 12. Ego : mē :: _____ : eam

    a. is   b. ea   c. tū   d. id

___ 13. Puella, cuī dōna dedimus, erat laeta.

        a. The girl, who gave us the gifts, was happy
        b. The girl, to whom we gave the gifts, was happy.
        c. We gave the gifts to the girl who was happy.
        d. The girl, whose gifts we received, was happy.

___ 14. Antonia, your brother will go <u>with you</u> to the butcher's shop.

        a. tēcum   b. vōs   c. vōbīscum   d. tibi

___ 15. Servus <u>grave onus</u> portāvit. Is_____in plaustrō posuit.

        a. illum   b. illa   c. illud   d. illīs

___ 16. He gave the trunks <u>to the slave women</u>.

        a. eī   b. eās   c. eārum   d. eīs

___ 17. Fābulae <u>of these women</u> vērae nōn sunt.

        a. hārum   b. huius   c. huic   d. hōrum

___ 18. Caupō, <u>with whom</u> pernoctāverāmus, erat amīcus nostrī paedagōgī.

        a. quācum   b. quibuscum   c. quōcum   d. quem

___ 19. _____ prope popīnam occurram.

        a. Hī   b. Huic   c. Hōs   d. Hanc

___ 20. Dominus multa mandāta servīs dedit, sed illī_____ nōn fēcērunt.

        a. eae   b. hoc   c. id   d. ea

PART 3

Adjectives and Adverbs

CHAPTER I — FORMS OF ADJECTIVES

IDENTIFICATION OF ADJECTIVE DECLENSIONS

In many ways adjectives are very similar to nouns. Just as with nouns, the four most important facts about adjectives are **case**, **gender**, **number**, and **declension**. Latin adjectives can be divided into two groups: those that belong to the 1st-2nd declensions, and those that belong to the 3rd declension.

1) 1st-2nd Declension Adjectives can be identified by their Nominative Singular endings of **-us** (masculine), **-a** (feminine), **-um** (neuter) or **-er** (masculine), **-ra** (feminine), **-rum** (neuter). Some examples of 1st-2nd declension Adjectives are:

magn**us**, mag**na**, mag**num**	*large*
pulch**er**, pulch**ra**, pulch**rum**	*beautiful*
līb**er**, līb**era**, līb**erum**	*free*

2) 3rd Declension Adjectives can be identified by their Nominative Singular endings of **-is** (masculine), **-is** (feminine), **-e** (neuter) or **-er** (masculine), **-ris** (feminine), **-re** (neuter). Other 3rd declension Adjectives have a Nominative Singular endings of **-x** (masculine, feminine, and neuter) or **-ns** (masculine, feminine, and neuter). Some examples of 3rd declension Adjectives are:

fort**is**, fort**is**, fort**e**	*brave, strong*
cel**er**, cel**eris**, cel**ere**	*fast, swiift*
ac**er**, ac**ris**, ac**re**	*bitter*
audā**x**	*bold*
intelligē**ns**	*intelligent*

PRACTICE ONE

Identify whether each of the following adjectives belongs to the 1st-2nd declensions or to the 3rd declension. Then circle and label the masculine, feminine, and neuter Nominative Singular endings of each adjective.

_____ 1. dēfessus, dēfessa, dēfessum

_____ 2. gravis, gravis, grave

_____ 3. ferōx

_____ 4. parvus, parva, parvum

_____ 5. prūdēns

_____ 6. omnis, omnis, omne

_____ 7. potēns

_____ 8. facilis, facilis, facile

_____ 9. miser, misera, miserum

_____ 10. laetus, laeta, laetum

_____ 11. tardus, tarda, tardum

_____ 12. acer, acris, acre

PRACTICE TWO

Look up the following adjectives in the dictionary at the back of the book. In the blanks provided, write out the feminine and neuter Nominative Singular forms of each adjective. Finally, identify whether each adjective belongs the the 1st-2nd declensions or to the 3rd declension. The first one is done for you.

1. cārus   cara   carum   1st-2nd

2. dīligēns _____ _____ _____

3. ērudītus _____ _____ _____

4. celer _____ _____ _____

5. fēlīx _____ _____ _____

6. ōbēsus _____ _____ _____

7. pīnguis _____ _____ _____

8. ēgregius _____ _____ _____

9. vehemēns _____ _____ _____

10. aequus _____ _____ _____

11. scelestus _____ _____ _____

12. pulcher _____ _____ _____

13. trīstis _____ _____ _____

14. vēlōx _____ _____ _____

15. alacer _____ _____ _____

16. difficilis _____ _____ _____

17. ferōx _____ _____ _____

18. meus _____ _____ _____

19. timidus _____ _____ _____

20. noster _____ _____ _____

FORMS OF ADJECTIVES

We will now review the forms for all cases of 1st-2nd and 3rd declension Adjectives.
Look at the chart below:

	1st-2nd Declension Adjectives			3rd Declension Adjectives	
SING.	*m.*	*f.*	*n.*	*m. & f.*	*n.*
Nom.	magnus	magna	magnum	omnis	omne
Gen.	magnī	magnae	magnī	omnis	omnis
Dat.	magnō	magnae	magnō	omnī	omnī
Acc.	magnum	magnam	magnum	omnem	omne
Abl.	magnō	magnā	magnō	omnī	omnī
PL.					
Nom.	magnī	magnae	magna	omnēs	omnia
Gen.	magnōrum	magnārum	magnōrum	omnium	omnium
Dat.	magnīs	magnīs	magnīs	omnibus	omnibus
Acc.	magnōs	magnās	magna	omnēs	omnia
Abl.	magnīs	magnīs	magnīs	omnibus	omnibus

NOTA BENE:

The endings of 1st -2nd declension Adjectives are identical to that of 1st and 2nd declension nouns.

The endings of 3rd declension Adjectives are identical to that of 3rd declension nouns **except:**
The Ablative Singular ending is **-ī** instead of **-e.**
The Nominative and Accusative neuter plural forms are **-ia.**
The Genitive Plural ending of all 3rd declension Adjectives is **-ium.**

PRACTICE THREE

*On a separate sheet of paper, complete adjective declension charts for the following
adjectives. Use the adjective declension chart above as your guide.*

1. parvus, parva, parvum
2. celer, celeris, celere
3. tardus, tarda, tardum
4. ingēns
5. pulcher, pulchra, pulchrum
6. fortis, fortis, forte

CHAPTER II — NOUN - ADJECTIVE AGREEMENT
. . . .

THE AGREEMENT OF NOUNS AND ADJECTIVES

An adjective in a Latin sentence must have the same case, gender, and number as the noun that it is modifying or describing. However, this agreement does **not** mean that this adjective will **always** have the same ending as the noun it modifies. The actual ending of the adjective will come from the declension to which it belongs. Look at the following examples.

1. <u>Puellam</u> (1st declen.) **laetam** spectō.   *I see the **happy** girl.*

2. <u>Puerum</u> (2nd declen.) **laetum** spectō.   *I see the **happy** boy.*

3. <u>Mīlitem</u> (3rd declen.) **laetum** spectō.   *I see the **happy** soldier.*

4. <u>Puellam</u> (1st declen.) **fortem** spectō.   *I see the **brave** girl.*

5. <u>Puerum</u> (2nd declen.) **fortem** spectō.   *I see the **brave** boy.*

6. <u>Mīlitem</u> (3rd declen.) **fortem** spectō.   *I see the **brave** soldier.*

The adjective **laetus, -a, -um** belongs to the 1st-2nd family of adjectives. Therefore in examples #1 and 2, since nouns of the 1st and 2nd declensions are being modified by a 1st and 2nd declension adjective, the noun and adjective share the same ending. In example #3, since the noun belongs to the 3rd declension, the noun and adjective do not share the same ending.

The adjective **fortis, -is, -e** belongs to the 3rd family of adjectives. Therefore in examples #4 and 5, since nouns of the 1st and 2nd declensions are being modified by a 3rd declension adjective, the noun and adjective do not share the same ending. In example #6, since the noun belongs to the 3rd declension, the noun and adjective share the same ending.

A full understanding of noun-adjective agreement is very important because the ending of an adjective describing a certain noun will not always be identical to the noun ending. Also remember that in Latin (especially poetry) the adjective may not be next to or even close to its noun.

The following practices will help you to understand better the grammatical relationship between nouns and adjectives.

Catullus 43
"You Are No Beauty Compared to My Girl"

Salvē, nec <u>minimō</u> puella nāsō
nec <u>bellō</u> pede nec <u>nigrīs</u> ocellīs
nec <u>longīs</u> digitīs nec ōre <u>siccō</u>
nec sānē nimis <u>ēlegānte</u> linguā.
Dēcoctōris amīca Formiānī,   5
tēn prōvincia nārrat esse <u>bellam</u>?
Tēcum Lesbia <u>nostra</u> comparātur?
Ō saeclum <u>insapiēns</u> et <u>īnfacētum</u>

nec	*not*	dēcoctor, -ōris, m.	*playboy, rake*
minimus, -a, -um	*very small*	Formiānus, -a, -um	*from Formiae*
niger, nigra, nigrum	*dark*	tēn = tē + nē	
ocellus, -ī, m.	*little eye*	comparātur	*she is compared*
ōs, ōris, n.	*mouth*	saeculum, -ī, n.	*generation, age*
siccus, -a, -um	*dry*	insapiēns, -ntis	*tasteless*
sānē	*clearly*	īnfacētus, -a, -um	*crude, witless*

NOTA BENE:
   In line four the adjective **ēlegante** has an Abl. sing. ending of **-e** instead of **-ī**.

PRACTICE ONE

In the poem above, all the adjectives have been underlined. By looking carefully at the poem, match all the adjectives with the nouns or pronouns that they modify. You will not use all the answers given and some answers may be used more than once.

_____1. minimō

_____2. bellō

_____3. nigrīs

_____4. longīs

_____5. siccō

_____6. ēlegānte

_____7. bellam

_____8. nostra

_____9. insapiēns

___10. infacētum

a. linguā

b. saeclum

c. puellā

d. tē

e. prōvincia

f. Lesbia

g. nāsō

h. ōre

i. pede

j. amīca

k. ocellīs

l. Formianī

m. tēcum

n. digitīs

How Proserpina Became the Queen of Hades

Dum petit in terrā Siculā Prōserpina flōrēs,
    errat ab ancillīs saepe puella suīs;
nam, "Prope nōn flōs est pulcherrimus," inquit, "amīcae.
    Saepe in dēsertōs īre necesse locōs."
Sōla olim sōlīs in agrīs dēfessa puella   5
    (heu!) sedet, et flōrem multum habet atque bonum,
cum prope sub parvā magnum videt arbore flōrem
    et petit. At flōrem nōn superāre potest.
Tum magis atque magis Prōserpina parva labōrat
    strēnua — sed frūstrā! Flōs magis haeret ibi.   10
Ecce! Puella, cavē! Mōnstrum est! Temerāria, mōnstrum
    (esque sine ancillīs sōla), puella, cavē!
At subitō parva est dīscissa sub arbore terra,
    appārent atrī quattuor intus equī.
"Ancillae, ferte auxilium!" Prōserpina clāmat,   15
    "Māter," et "auxilium fer, dea magna, mihi!
Dīs mē habet!" At cēlat lacrimantem terra puellam.
    Invenit et dominam servula nūlla suam.

terra, -ae, f.	*earth, ground*	**superāre**	*to overcome*
Siculus, -a, -um	*Sicilian*	**magis**	*more*
flōs, flōris, m.	*flower*	**mōnstrum, -ī, n.**	*warning*
pulcherrimus, -a, um	*very beautiful*	**est dīscissa**	*was torn apart*
locus, -ī, m.	*place*	**ater, atra, atrum**	*black*
olim	*one day*	**intus**	*inside*
heu	*alas*	**Dīs, Dītis, m.**	*Dis, god of the underworld*
atque	*and*		
at	*but*	**servula, -ae, f.**	*slave girl*

Hecate triformis

PRACTICE TWO

The chart below lists all the adjectives found in the poem on page eighty-three. Complete the chart by listing what noun each adjective modifies and then give the meaning of the resulting phrase. The first one is done for you.

Adjective	Line # of adj.	Noun being modified	Line # of noun	meaning of noun-adjective phrase
1. Sicula	1	terra	1	on Sicilian ground
2. suīs	2			
3. pulcherrimus	3			
4. dēsertōs	4			
5. sōla	5			
6. sōlīs	5			
7. dēfessa	5			
8. multum	6			
9. bonum	6			
10. parvā	7			
11. magnum	7			
12. parva	9			
13. strēnua	10			
14. Temerāria	11			
15. sōla	12			
16. parva	13			
17. atrī	14			
18. magna	16			
19. lacrimantem	17			
20. nūlla	18			
21. suam	18			

PRACTICE THREE
Match the correct form of the adjective _noster, nostra, nostrum_ with the noun that it describes. You will not use all the answers.

____1. gladiātōrēs (acc.)   a. nostrī

____2. māter   b. noster

____3. urbis   c. nostrīs

____4. servī   d. nostram

____5. puellam   e. nostra

____6. senātōribus   f. nostrae

                                       g. nostrōs

PRACTICE FOUR
Match the correct form of the adjective _omnis, omnis, omne_ with the noun that it describes. You will not use all the answers.

____1. pictūram   a. omnibus

____2. pater   b. omnium

____3. flūmina   c. omne

____4. puerōrum   d. omnēs

____5. agrōs   e. omnem

____6. puellīs   f. omnis

                                       g. omnia

PRACTICE FIVE
For each underlined adjective in the following sentences, draw an arrow to the noun that it describes. Then translate the sentence into English.

1. Puer <u>dēfessōs</u> aurīgās in Circō spectat._____

_____

2. Puer <u>dēfessus</u> aurīgās in Circō spectat._____

_____

3. <u>Magnō</u> puerī aurīgās <u>paucī</u> in Circō spectant._____

_____

(cont.)

4. Senātor gravis epistulās scrībit._____

_____

5. Senātor gravēs epistulās scrībit._____

_____

6. Puella parva canem habet._____

_____

7. Puella parvum canem habet._____

_____

8. Magnum puella canem parva habet._____

_____

9. Ferōcēs mīles barbariōs fortis vulnerat._____

_____

10. Ferōcem barbarī fortēs mīlitem vulnerant._____

_____

PRACTICE SIX

Select the correct form of the adjective to complete the meaning of the sentence and write the letter of your answer in the space provided.

_____1. _____ pater multās epistulās scrībit.

    a. Mea   b. Meō   c. Meī   d. Meus

_____2. Ego _____ servōs videō.

    a. omnēs   b. omne   c. omnis   d. omnem

_____3. Cum _____ puellīs ambulātis.

    a. fortis   b. forte   c. fortī   d. fortibus

_____4. Numerus _____ gladiātōrum in arēnā erat magnus.

    a. mortuīs   b. mortuum   c. mortuōrum   d. mortuī

_____5. In _____ urbe multī hominēs habitant.

    a. magnā   b. magnī   c. magna   d. magne

_____6. _____ tempōre meī amīcī nōbīs auxilium ferent.

    a. Breve   b. Brevī   c. Brevis   d. Brevium

_____7. Pecūniam fūrī _____ nōn donābāmus.

    a. scelestīs   b. scelestī   c. scelestō   d. scelestōs

PRACTICE SEVEN
Circle the correct form of the adjective that agrees with each of the boldfaced nouns in the story below.

A Haunted House

Olim in **urbe** (Graeca, Graecā, Graecam) erat **villa** (spatiōsam, spatiōsae, spatiōsa)

et magna sed īnfāmis et (pestilentī, pestilentem, pestilēns). Nocte (perterritī,

perterritōs, perterritīs) **inhabitantēs** strepitum magnum **vinculōrum** (gravem,

gravium, gravis) in villā audiēbant. Mox apparēbat idolon, senex quī **crīnēs** (sordidī,

sordidō, sordidōs) et **barbam** (prōmissam, prōmissa, prōmissārum) habēbat. In   5

manibus crūribusque erant (gravibus, gravī, gravia) **vincula** quae senex quatiēbat.

Nunc **inhabitantēs** erant (miserōs, miserī, miserīs) quod maximē **idolon** (trīste,

trīstia, trīstium) timēbant.

(based on Pliny's Letters VII.27)

Graecus, -a, -um	*Greek*	**senex, senis, m.**	*old man*
īnfāmis, -e	*notorious*	**barba, -ae, f.**	*beard*
pestilēns, pestilentis	*infected*	**prōmissus, -a, um**	*growing long*
strepitus, -ūs, m.	*noise*	**crūs, crūris, n.**	*leg*
idolon, -ī, n.	*image, ghost*	**quatiēbat**	*he was shaking*

PRACTICE EIGHT
Based on the story above, answer the following questions in English.

1. Where was the house located?_____

   _____

2. What did the inhabitants hear at night?_____

   _____

3. Describe the appearance of the ghost._____

   _____

4. What were seen on the ghost's hands and legs?_____

   _____

5. Why were the inhabitants unhappy?_____

   _____

CHAPTER III — THE FORMATION AND USE OF ADVERBS

. . . .

HOW ADVERBS ARE USED

Adverbs commonly modify the verb in a sentence. However they can also modify adjectives or other adverbs. Whatever word an adverb modifies, it never changes its ending: adverbs **cannot** be declined. An adverb usually directly precedes the word that it modifies. An adverb in a sentence answers one of these questions: *when? why? where?* or *how?*

1) Adverb modifying a verb:
   Dominus servum **ferōciter** verberābat.   *The master **fiercely** beat the slave.*

2) Adverb modifying an adjective:
   Puer est **valdē** aeger.   *The boy is **seriously** ill.*

3) Adverb modifying another adverb:
   Nunc **quoque** eius māter est aegra.   *Now **also** his mother is ill.*

SOME COMMON ADVERBS FOUND IN LATIN

Adverbs fall into the general categories of *time* (when), *place* (where), and *manner* (how) Here are some common Latin adverbs listed by their category.

Adverbs of Time

cum	*when*	nunc	*now*
iam	*already*	quandō	*when?*
mox	*soon*	ubi	*when?*
cotīdiē	*every day*	saepe	*often*
crās	*tomorrow*	semper	*always*
herī	*yesterday*	numquam	*never*
hodiē	*today*	umquam	*ever*
diū	*for a long time*	noctē	*at night*
interdiū	*during the day*	quamdiū	*how long*
iterum	*again*	sērō	*late*
manē	*in the morning*	statim	*immediately*

Adverbs of Place

eō	*to that place*	inde	*from that place*
hīc	*here*	quō	*to what place*
hinc	*from this place*	ubi	*where*
ibi	*there*	unde	*from what place*

Adverbs of Manner

cur	*why*	**quam**	*how*
igitur	*therefore*	**quōmodo**	*how*
ita	*so*	**sic**	*so*
itaque	*therefore*	**tam**	*so*
paene	*almost*	**vix**	*scarcely*

PRACTICE ONE

Match these adverbs with their meanings. There are more choices than you will need.

____1. quandō

____2. quō

____3. hīc

____4. cur

____5. noctē

____6. nunc

____7. igitur

____8. iterum

____9. paene

__ 10. cotīdiē

a. today

b. at night

c. therefore

d. here

e. every day

f. when

g. now

h. to what place

i. almost

j. again

k. for a long time

l. why

PRACTICE TWO

Circle the adverb(s) in each sentence. Then answer each question with a complete sentence <u>in English</u> in the space provided.

1. Ībisne ad lūdum crās?_____

2. Nōnne semper lūdum amās?_____

3. Num manē surgere amās?_____

4. Quid herī fēcistī? _____

5. Unde tū lūdō appropīnquās?_____

6. Quid nunc facis?_____

(cont.)

7. Quō ībis ubi lūdum reliqueris?_____

8. Vīsne īre cubitum sērō?_____

9. Num tū cotīdiē in lūdō diū manēs?_____

10. Īvistīne tū ad lūdum umquam noctē?_____

HOW ADVERBS ARE FORMED FROM ADJECTIVES

Other adverbs are regularly formed from adjectives in the ways listed below:

First and Second Declension Adjectives add **-ē** to the base of the adjective to form the adverb.

Adjective	Base	Adverb	English Meaning
tardus	tard-	tardē	*slowly*
carus	car-	carē	*dearly*
līber	līber-	līberē	*freely*
pulcher	pulchr-	pulchrē	*beautifully*

Third Declension Adjectives add **-iter** to the base of the adjective to form the adverb. However Third Declension Adjectives that end in **-ns** add **-er** to the base of the adjective.

Adjective	Base	Adverb	English Meaning
fortis	fort-	fortiter	*bravely*
celer	celer-	celeriter	*swiftly*
acer	acr-	acriter	*bitterly*
fēlīx	fēlīc-	fēlīciter	*happily*
sapiēns	sapient-	sapienter	*wisely*

For adjectives that end in **-er** you can remember whether or not the base of the adjective keeps the entire **-er** by looking at an English derivative of the adjective:

Latin Adjective	English Derivative	Base
līber	liberty	līber-
celer	accelerate	celer-
pulcher	pulchritude	pulchr-
acer	acrid	acr-

The bases for Third Declension Adjectives are also easy to remember. Adjectives that end in **-is** drop the **-is** to form their base. Adjectives that end in **-x** change the final letter to **-c.** Adjectives that end in **-ns** change the final letters to **-nt.**

Latin Adjective	Base of Adjective
fortis	fort-
fēlīx	fēlīc-
sapiēns	sapient-

NOTA BENE:
   Bonus and **magnus** form adverbs irregularly: **bene,** *well;* **māgnopere,** *greatly*

PRACTICE THREE

Identify each adjective as belonging to the 1st-2nd or 3rd declension. Then form the adverb and translate the adverb into English. The first one is done for you.

Adjective	Declen # of Adj.	Form of Adverb	Meaning of Adverb
1. miser	1-2	miserē	sadly
2. ferōx			
3. aequus			
4. bonus			
5. prudēns			
6. gravis			
7. longus			
8. lātus			
9. altus			
10. vēlōx			
11. malus			
12. trīstis			
13. potēns			
14. magnus			
15. rēctus			

PRACTICE FOUR

From the pool of words below select and write the adverb in the blank that correctly
completes the meaning of the sentence. You will not use all the adverbs listed.

1. Quod domina erat īrāta, eius ancillae _____ eī appropīnquabant.

2. Quod aurīga vīctōriam habet, Antōnius nōmen _____ clāmat.

3. Quod dominus vīlicum vidēre vult, ex agrīs in villam _____ it.

4. Quod Caesar est imperātōr, omnēs mīlitēs _____ pugnābunt.

5. Ubi puerī sunt malī, pater eōs _____ pūnit.

celeriter	laetē	procāciter
timidē	fortiter	aeque

PRACTICE FIVE

In each of the following pairs of sentences, form an adverb from the adjective underlined
in the first sentence and write the adverb in the blank provided in the second sentence.
Then translate both sentences. The first one is done for you.

1. Antōnius <u>magnā</u> vōce nōmen aurīgae clāmat. Ille **magnopere** commovetur quod
   aurīga vīctōriam nōn habet. <u>Antonius shouts the name of the charioteer in a</u>
   <u>loud voice. He is greatly upset because the charioteer does not win.</u>

2. Antōnius responsum <u>rēctum</u> magistrō dat. Magistrō placet quod discipulus
   _____ respondit._____

   _____

   _____

3. <u>Dīligentēs</u> servae stolās dominae parant. Stolās in cistam _____ pōnunt. ____

   _____

   _____

4. <u>Laetī</u> līberī cantant. Māter līberōrum_____ audit. _____

   _____

5. Tabellārius equōs <u>celerēs</u> per viam agit. Tabellārius epistulās ad villam senātōris
   _____ fert. _____

   _____

CHAPTER IV — REVIEW OF ADJECTIVES AND ADVERBS

· ·

SUMMARY OF ADJECTIVES AND ADVERBS

1) Adjectives can be declined and must agree in gender, case, and number with the noun that they describe. Adjective may belong to either the 1st and 2nd declension or to the 3rd declension.

2) Adverbs **cannot** be declined. They modify verbs, adjectives and other adverbs. An adverb in a sentence answers one of these questions: *when? why? where?* or *how?*

3) An adverb is regularly formed from the base of its adjective. For 1st and 2nd declension adjectives add **-ē** to the base. For 3rd declension adjectives add **-iter** (or **-er** if the base ends in **-nt**).

PRACTICE ONE

Read through the story below and circle all the adjectives and underline all the adverbs.

Pliny's wife Calpurnia was the niece of Calpurnia Hispulla. Calpurnia Hispulla had raised her niece and helped to arrange her marriage to Pliny. In this letter Pliny is thanking Calpurnia Hispulla for rearing such a gentile young lady.

Thank You for My Wife

Tibi gaudium magnum erit. Mea uxor, Calpurnia minor, est dīgna patre, dīgna tē, dīgna avō. Puella summum acūmen et frūgālitātem summam habet. Māgnoperē mē amat. Hic amor mihi est iūdicium castitātis. Puella meōs libellōs habet, eōs semper lēctitat, etiam bene ēdiscit.

Quam sollicita est ubi domō relinquō et ad Curiam eō. Quam laeta est ubi domum   5
reveniō. Nūntiōs saepe ad Forum dispōnit. Nūntiī celeriter domum reveniunt et eī dē ēventō ōrātiōnum nārrant. Ubi mea carmina recitō, puella discrēta vēlō sedet et meās laudēs avidē audit. Quīdem meōs versus dīligenter cantat et etiam citharā fōrmat.

Ego spem magnam habet quod noster amor est validus. Diēs nostrī cōnūbiī certē erunt longī. Puella nōn aetātem aut corpus quae paulatim senescent, sed ēgregiam   10
glōriam dīligit. Haec puella vītam sapienter agit quod in contuberniō tuō nihil nisi sanctum honestumque vidit. Ego et mea uxor tibi maximās grātiās agimus.

(based on Pliny's Letters IV. 19)

minor, minus	*younger*	**frūgālitās, -tātis, f.**	*thrift, economy*
dīgnus, -a, -um + abl.	*worthy*	**iūdicium, -ī, n.**	*indication*
summus, -a, -um	*highest*	**castitās, -tātis, f.**	*moral purity*

(cont.)

acūmen, -inis, n.	keeness	libellus, -ī, m.	little book
lēctitat	she recites	spes, speī, f.	hope
ēdiscit	she memorizes	cōnūbium, -ī, n.	marriage
ēventus, -ūs, m.	outcome	aetās, aetātis, f.	youth
ōrātiō, -ōnis, f.	speech, oration	ēgregius, -a, -um	outstanding
discrētus, -a, -um	hidden	contubernium, -ī, n.	company
vēlum, -ī, n.	curtain	māximus, -a, -um	greatest
avidus, -a, -um	eargerly		
citharā fōrmat	plays on the cithara		

PRACTICE TWO

On a separate sheet of paper, _in English_, summarize in your own words what qualities of the younger Calpurnia made her so appealing as a wife to Pliny.

PRACTICE THREE

Match the Latin adjective or adverb with its correct English meaning. You will not use all of your answers.

____1. timidus

____2. cur

____3. gravis

____4. ferōciter

____5. miserē

____6. vēlōx

____7. saepe

____8. prudēns

____9. laetus

___10. timidē

___11. dīligenter

___12. magnus

a. great

b. swift

c. wisely

d. happy

e. often

f. painstakingly

g. fierce

h. sadly

i. serious

j. fearful

k. greatly

l. wise

m. when

n. fiercely

o. why

p. fearfully

PRACTICE FOUR

From the pool of names below match each description with the correct mythological hero or heroine. You will not use any answer more than once.

_____1. Diū uxōrem et fīlium nōn vīdī. Mea fidēlis uxor vīgintī annōs meum reditum ad Ithacam dīligenter exspectābat.

_____2. Ego sum vir magnus et ferōx. Nōlīte umquam mē īrātum facēre. Ego duodecim dūrōs labōrēs confēcī.

_____3. Ego sum pulchra fēmina. Omnēs ducēs in Graeciā mē uxōrem cupiēbant. Sed Trōiānus vir audācter mē cēpit et Trōiam dūxit.

_____4.. Ego sum vir parvus sed intelligēns. In Cretā ferōx mōnstrum fortiter occidī.

_____5. Ego celeriter per agrōs meī patris currere amō. Ego marītum habēre nōlō. In certāminibus nēmō mē vincere potest. Sed puer sapiēns auxiliō deae et trium aureōrum malōrum nunc mē vīcit.

_____6. Ego nōn sum Graeca sed barbara fēmina. Meus marītus novam Graecam uxōrem in mātrimōnium ducere nunc vult. Igitur crās meōs duōs līberōs interficiam.

Medea	Helen of Troy	Odysseus
Hercules	Perseus	Atalanta
Daphne	Theseus	Jason

PRACTICE FIVE

Select the best answer from a, b, c, or d. Write your answer in the blanks provided.

____1. Scrībe <u>often</u> mihi.

    a. bonum   b. malum   c. cur   d. saepe

____2. Estne noster dux <u>smart</u>?

    a. intelligenter   b. intelligentēs   c. intelligēns   d. intelligentem

____3. The charioteer is <u>sad</u> because he has lost the race.

    a. misera   b. miserum   c. miseram   d. miser

____4. Servus <u>heavy</u> plaustrum sine auxiliō equōrum movēre nōn potest.

    a. gravēs   b. gravia   c. graviter   d. grave

____5. Jupiter est <u>powerful</u> deus.

    a. potentēs   b. potenter   c. potēns   d. potentia

(cont.)

_____6. <u>Fearfully</u> the slaves gather to hear the overseer speak.

    a. Timidī   b. Timidē   c. Timidus   d. Timidōs

_____7. The <u>industrious</u> servī in agrīs diū labōrābant.

    a. dīligentī   b. dīligēns   c. dīligenter   d. dīligentēs

_____8. The ghost of Hector <u>mournfully</u> stood before Aeneas.

    a. maestus   b. maestī   c. maestum   d. maestē

_____9. Aeneas gazed at the <u>serious</u> wounds that covered Hector's body.

    a. gravium   b. gravia   c. gravēs   d. gravī

___10. "O long <u>awaited</u> Hector, from what shores do you arrive?" said Aeneas.

    a. exspectātus   b. exspectāta   c. exspectāte   d. exspectātī

___11. Praeclārus senātor prīncipem <u>truly</u> laudat.

    a. verē   b. verīs   c. verōs   d. veram

___12. Why do you walk <u>so</u> slowly to school?

    a. igitur   b. etiam   c. tam   d. valdē

___13. Gladiātōrēs in arēnā <u>bravely</u> pugnant.

    a. fortiter   b. fortium   c. fortibus   d. fortis

___14. <u>Why</u> do you dislike the master?

    a. Cūr   b. Quando   c. Ubi   d. Umquam

___15. Clāmōrēs <u>of the happy</u> līberōrum audiēbāmus.

    a. fēlicium   b. fēlicēs   c. fēlicī   d. fēlicis

___16. Pater <u>good</u> vīnum bibere amat.

    a. bene   b. bona   c. bonum   d. bonā

___17. Pater, nōlī vīnum <u>quickly</u> bibere!

    a. celere   b. celeriter   c. celeria   d. celeris

___18. The senator gave an <u>excellent</u> speech.

    a. ēgregiam   b. ēgregius   c. ēgregium   d. egregiae

___19. Sapiēns : sapienter :: magnus : _____ .

    a. magnō   b. māgnopere   c. magis   d. magnē

___20. Ego leōnēs et tigrēs <u>strongly</u> timeō.

    a. valdē   b. valdī   c. valdōrum   d. valdam

PART 4

Verbs - Active Voice
CHAPTER I — BASIC INFORMATION ABOUT VERBS

WHAT ARE VERBS?

A verb is an essential part of any sentence. Every sentence must have one. The verb tells you what the subject (a noun, pronoun, or implied subject) is doing. To understand what a verb is trying to tell you about the subject of a sentence you must consider the following facts about each Latin verb.

1) **Person** - the point of view of the subject of the sentence.

   1st person - The subject of the sentence is talking about him or herself.

Fābulam **nārrō**.	*I tell a story.*
Fābulam **nārrāmus**.	*We tell a story.*

   2nd person - Someone is talking directly to the subject of the sentence.

Fābulam **nārrās**.	*You (s.) tell a story.*
Fābulam **nārrātis**.	*You (pl.) tell a story.*

   3rd person - Someone is talking about the subject of the sentence.

Fābulam **nārrat**.	*He tells a story.*
Fābulam **nārrant**.	*They tell a story.*

2) **Number** - refers to whether a verb is singular or plural.

Singular	Fābulam **nārrō**.	*I tell a story.*
Plural	Fābulam **nārrāmus**.	*We tell a story.*

3) **Tense**- refers to the time the action of the verb takes place: Present, Future, or Past.

Present Tense	Fābulam **nārro**.	*I tell a story.*
Future Tense	Fābulam **nārrābō**.	*I will tell a story.*
Past Tense	Fābulam **nārrābam**.	*I was telling a story.*

4) **Conjugation** - refers to the family to which a verb belongs. The verb conjugation determines what vowels are used to link the stem of the verb to the personal ending of the verb. The same vowel can mean a different tense depending on to which conjugation the verb belongs.

Present	Villam videt (2nd conjugation)	*He sees a house.*
Future	Villam petet (3rd conjugation)	*He will find the house.*

5) **Voice** - refers to whether the subject is doing the action (active voice) or whether the subject is being acted upon (passive voice). In Part IV we will review only verbs that are in the active voice.

Active Voice	Puer nūntium **salvat**.	*The boy **greets** the messenger.*
Passive Voice	Puer ā nūntiō **salvatur**.	*The boy **is greeted** by the messenger.*

6) **Mood** - refers to how the verb is being used in a sentence. In Part IV we will review three possible moods of verbs. The **indicative** mood is used for verbs that are stating or asking a fact. The **imperative** mood is used for verbs that are giving a command. The **infinitive** mood is used when a verb is acting as a verbal noun.

Indicative	Servus vestīmenta **custōdit**.	*The slave **guards** the clothes.*
Indicative	Servusne vestīmenta **custōdit**?	*Is the slave **guarding** the clothes?*
Imperative	Serve, vestīmenta custōdī!	*Slave, **guard** the clothes.*
Infinitive	Vestīmenta **custōdīre** est labor servī.	***To guard** clothes is the task of a slave.*

IDENTIFYING VERB CONJUGATIONS

When you look up verbs in a Latin dictionary you will most often find four forms listed for the verbs. These four forms are called the principal parts of a verb because all other forms of the verb will be created from one of these four forms.

spectō, spectāre, spectāvī, spectātus, *to see*

faciō, facere, fēcī, factus, *to make*

For now, we will just review the first two principal parts of the verb. These first two principal parts of any Latin verb help you to identify to which verb conjugation a verb belongs. There are four regular verb conjugations in Latin. All second principal parts of regular verbs end in **-re**. It is the vowel **before** the -re that determines the verb conjugation.

The 2nd and 3rd conjugation endings on the second principal part of verbs are identical except for the quantity or length of the vowel preceding the final **-re.** For 2nd conjugation the vowel is always a **long e,** for 3rd conjugation always a **short e.**

3rd conjugation verbs come in two varieties — **3rd and 3rd io**. Look at the first principal part of a 3rd conjugation verb to see which variety it is.

spectō, spectāre	1st conjugation
doceō, docēre	2nd conjugation
petō, petere	3rd conjugation
capiō, capere	3rd io conjugation
audiō, audīre	4th conjugation

PRACTICE ONE

Circle the vowel + re in the infinitive that identifies each verb conjugation. Then write the verb conjugation I, II, III, IIIio, or IV in the blank for each of the following verbs.

_____1. audiō audīre   _____5. ascendō ascendere   _____9. pugnō pugnāre

_____2. maneō manēre   _____6. conspiciō conspicere   _____10. nūntiō nūntiāre

_____3. saliō salīre   _____7. clāmō clāmāre   _____11. puniō punīre

_____4. teneō tenēre   _____8. dīcō dīcere   _____12. capiō capere

PRACTICE TWO

Using the Latin to English dictionary at the back of this book, write out the correct infinitive form for each of the following verbs. Then identify the conjugation of each verb. The first one is done for you.

<u>1st</u>___ 1. nārrō nārr   <u>nārrāre</u>   _____6. regō reg   _____

_____2. moneō mon   _____   _____7. incipiō incip   _____

_____3. faciō fac   _____   _____8. veniō ven   _____

_____4. orō or   _____   _____9. currō curr   _____

_____5. muniō mun   _____   _____10. timeō tim   _____

SUBJECT-VERB AGREEMENT

The subject and main verb in a sentence must agree in **person (1st, 2nd, or 3rd)** and in **number (singular or plural)**. In English the subject of the sentence is expressed with a noun or pronoun.

Antonia sings.	Antōnia canta**t**.
She sings.	Canta**t**.
Antonia and Claudia sing.	Antōnia et Claudia canta**nt**.
They sing.	Canta**nt**.

In Latin, the personal ending on the verb, in this example **-t** or **-nt**, indicates the person and number of the subject of the sentence. The subject of a verb is regularly expressed by a noun, but Latin can also use personal pronouns to express the subject. The following chart will help you remember the verb endings and the corresponding personal pronouns.

Personal Verb Endings					
SINGULAR			PLURAL		
English Pronoun	Latin Verb Ending	Latin Pronoun	English Pronoun	Latin Verb Ending	Latin Pronoun
I	-ō (m)	Ego	We	-mus	Nōs
You	-s	Tū	You	-tis	Vōs
He, She, It	-t	Is, Ea, Id	They	-nt	Eī, Eae, Ea

NOTA BENE:

The 1st person sing. has an alternate ending **-m** that is used where an **-ō** at the end of the verb would be difficult to pronounce. Examples: dūcō - I lead, but dūcam - I will lead, and dūcēbam, I was leading.

Latin has no real 3rd person personal pronouns. Most often forms of the demonstrative pronouns **is, hic** or **ille** are used.

Often the ending of the verb is the only clue to establishing the identity of the verb's subject.

PRACTICE THREE

In the following sentences the subjects appear in boldface. Indicate the person and number of the subject in the blanks provided. Underline the personal ending on the verb. Then translate the sentence into English. All verbs are in the present tense. The first one has been done for you.

	Person	Number
1. **Vōs** es<u>tis</u> meī amīcī.	2nd	Plural

You are my friends.

2. **Ego** multōs amīcōs habeō.

3. Hodiē **servī** in agrīs labōrant.

4. Cūr **gladiātor** pugnāre nōn vult?

5. **Nōs** ad forum ambulāmus.

6. Quō **pater** et **patruus** eunt?

7. Quid faciunt **mīlitēs**?   _____   _____

_____

8. **Tūne** novum coquum habēs?   _____   _____

_____

9. **Ego** et **māter** fābulam patris audīmus.   _____   _____

_____

10. Cūr, **ancilla**, nōn festīnās?   _____   _____

_____

11. Hodiē **animālia** in Circō ferōcia sunt.   _____   _____

_____

PRACTICE FOUR

Circle the personal verb endings of each of the following verbs. Then from the pool of nouns and pronouns select the correct one to agree with the verb form and write it in the blanks provided. You may use an answer more than once.

_____1. cantāmus   _____6. curritis

_____2. fert   _____7. dormis

_____3. faciunt   _____8. sedeō

_____4. incitant   _____9. ambulō

_____5. possum   _____10. īmus

Ego	Tū	Puella
Nōs	Vōs	Puellae

PRACTICE FIVE

All the following verb forms are in the present tense. Circle the personal verb ending for each of the following verbs. Then translate each verb form into English.

1. surgimus _____

2. excitant _____

3. induō _____

4. currimus _____

5. terrēs _____

6. petitis _____

7. salūtat _____

8. capitis _____

9. sumus _____

10. estis _____

11. scrībunt _____

12. sum _____

13. legō _____

14. labōrat _____

15. dūcis _____

16. vocāmus _____

17. advenis _____

18. errō _____

19. timent _____

20. docet _____

CHAPTER II — THE PRESENT TENSE

. . . .

THE FORMATION OF THE PRESENT TENSE

The Present tense of regular verbs is formed from the present stem of the verb. The present stem is the second principal part of the verb minus the -re ending. To the present stem you add the personal verb endings -ō (-m), -s, -t, -mus, -tis, -nt. In the following examples the present stem is underlined

I	II	III	IIIio	IV
amō, amāre	doceō, docēre	regō, regere	capiō, capere	muniō, munīre
amō	doceō	regō	capiō	muniō
amās	docēs	regis	capis	munīs
amat	docet	regit	capit	munit
amāmus	docēmus	regimus	capimus	munīmus
amātis	docētis	regitis	capitis	munītis
amant	docent	regunt	capiunt	muniunt

Notice that for each verb conjugation there is a vowel that links the stem of the verb to the personal verb endings.

1st conjugation - the linking vowel is a **long -a**. In the first person singular the **long -a** is swallowed   up by the personal verb ending **-ō**.

2nd conjugation - the linking vowel is a **long -e**. The **long -e** is not affected by the consonants that follow.

3rd conjugation - the linking vowel is a **short -e**. When a **short -e** is followed by a consonant it turns to a **short -i**. A **short -i** followed by **-nt** turns to **-u**.

3rd io conjugation - the rules for the linking vowel for 3rd conjugation verbs still apply. However in the 1st person singular the **short -i** is not swallowed up by the personal verb ending **-ō**. In the 3rd person plural the linking vowels become **-iu**.

4th conjugation - the linking vowel is a **long -i**. The **long -i** is is not affected by the consonants that follow.

NOTA BENE:
 The following little saying will help you to remember the difference between the 2nd and 3rd conjugations:
 2nd conjugation verbs say: We have a **long -e** that is strong and never disappears or changes.
 3rd conjugations verbs say: We have a **short -e** that is weak and helpless. It changes to **-i** when followed by another vowel or consonant.

HOW TO TRANSLATE THE PRESENT TENSE

The Latin present tense form **ambulat** can be translated into English three different ways. It is up to you to decide which is the best English translation by looking at the context of the sentence within the paragraph or story.

Puella in agrīs **ambulat**.	*The girl **walks** in the fields.*	Simple Present
	*The girl **is walking** in the fields.*	Progressive Present
	*The girl **does walk** in the fields.*	Emphatic Present

NOTA BENE:
 Note that Latin does not use a helping verb for **is** or **does**.

PRACTICE ONE

Complete the present tense conjugation charts for each of the following verbs. Use the model verbs on page one hundred and three as your guide.

	agō, agere	finiō, finīre	laudō, laudāre
1st. sing.		finiō	
2nd sing.	agis		
3rd. sing.			
1st pl.			
2nd pl.			laudātis
3rd pl.			

	accipiō, accipere	rideō, ridēre	dūcō, dūcere
1st. sing.			
2nd sing.			
3rd. sing.		ridet	
1st pl.			dūcimus
2nd pl.			
3rd pl.	accipiunt		

PRACTICE TWO
Change each of the following verb forms from singular to plural.

1. spectās   _____
2. excipiō   _____
3. portō   _____
4. agit   _____
5. induis   _____

6. facit   _____
7. vidēs   _____
8. incipiō   _____
9. salutās   _____
10. advenit   _____

PRACTICE THREE
Change each of the following verb forms from plural to singular.

1. postulāmus _____
2. vocant   _____
3. interficitis _____
4. tenēmus   _____
5. munītis   _____

6. aspiciunt _____
7. movētis   _____
8. timent   _____
9. errant   _____
10. capimus _____

PRACTICE FOUR
Translate each of the following sentences into English using three different translations of the present tense verb. The first one is done for you.

1. Antōnius cum amīcīs ambulat.

   <u>Antonius walks with his friends.</u>

   <u>Antonius is walking with his friends.</u>

   <u>Antonius does walk with his friends.</u>

2. Cotīdiē puella lānam trahit.   (lānam trahere - *to spin wool*)

   _____

   _____

   _____

3. Puerī in flūmine natant.

   _____

   _____

   _____

(cont.)

4. Servī, in parvīs cubiculīs dormītis.

_____

_____

_____

5. Diū in forō maneō.

_____

_____

_____

6. In arēnā gladiatōrēs cōnspicimus.

_____

_____

_____

7. Senātor, longum iter facis.

_____

_____

_____

CHAPTER III — THE IMPERFECT TENSE
. . . .

THE FORMATION OF THE IMPERFECT TENSE

The imperfect tense of regular verbs is formed by adding the tense sign **-bā-** to the present stem which is underlined in the examples below. Next you place the personal verb endings **-m, -s, -t, -mus, -tis, -nt**. Note that each verb conjugation has a **linking vowel or vowels** that connect the base of the verb to the tense sign and personal endings. In the following examples the **linking vowel(s)** and **-bā- tense signs** are boldfaced.

I amō, <u>amā</u>re	II doceō, <u>docē</u>re	III regō, <u>rege</u>re	IIIio capiō, <u>cape</u>re	IV muniō, <u>munī</u>re
amābam	docēbam	regēbam	capiēbam	muniēbam
amābās	docēbās	regābās	capiēbās	muniēbās
amabat	docebat	regebat	capiebat	muniebat
amābāmus	docēbāmus	regēbāmus	capiēbāmus	muniēbāmus
amābātis	docēbātis	regēbātis	capiēbātis	muniēbātis
amābant	docēbant	regēbant	capiēbant	muniēbant

Remember that the 1st singular personal (verb) ending of the imperfect tense is **-m** instead of **-ō**.

The following chart will help you to remember the linking vowels and tense sign combination for each verb conjugation.

I **-ābā-**	II **-ēbā-**	III **-ēbā-**	IIIio **-iēbā-**	IV **-iēbā-**

NOTA BENE:
   The following saying will help you to remember the tense sign for the imperfect tense.
   Ba Ba black sheep! Do you know your imperfect? Yes sir, yes sir, we sure do.

HOW TO TRANSLATE THE IMPERFECT TENSE

The imperfect tense is used in Latin to denote a continuous or incompleted action that occurred in the past. There are a number of ways to translate the Latin imperfect tense into English. It is up to you to decide which is the best English translation by looking at the context of the sentence within the paragraph or story.

Puella in agrīs **ambulābat**.

*The girl **walked** in the fields.*

*The girl **was walking** in the fields.*

*The girl **used to walk** in the fields.*

*The girl **began to walk** in the fields.*

*The girl **kept on walking** in the fields.*

NOTA BENE:
  Note that Latin, unlike English, does not use any helping verbs in the imperfect tense.

PRACTICE ONE

Complete the conjugation charts of the imperfect tense for each of the following verbs.
Use the model verbs on page one hundred and seven as your guide.

	moveō, movēre	efficiō, efficere	pōnō, pōnere
1st. sing.			
2nd sing.			
3rd. sing.			
1st pl.			
2nd pl.			
3rd pl.			

	ēdūcō, ēdūcere	aperiō, aperīre	incitō, incitāre
1st. sing.			
2nd sing.			
3rd. sing.			
1st pl.			
2nd pl.			
3rd pl.			

PRACTICE TWO

Change each of the following verbs in the present tense to the imperfect tense, keeping the same person and number. The conjugation of the verb is listed in parentheses.

1. errant (1) _____
2. terret (2) _____
3. facis (3io) _____
4. petimus (3) _____
5. munītis (4) _____

6. amāmus (1) _____
7. geritis (3) _____
8. clamō (1) _____
9. invenit (4) _____
10. manēs (2) _____

PRACTICE THREE

Make each verb imperfect by adding the correct linking vowel, tense sign and personal ending. Be sure that you have subject-verb agreement. Then translate each sentence into English using two different translations of the imperfect tense. The first one is done for you.

1. Antōnius vidēbat__. Antonius saw. Antonius used to see. _____

_____

2. Nōs inven_____. _____

_____

3. Tū port_____. _____

_____

4. Vōs ag_____. _____

_____

5. Nōs aud_____. _____

_____

6. Carrus mov_____. _____

_____

7. Ego dorm_____. _____

_____

(cont.)

8. Puellae cant_____. _____

    _____

9. Senatōrēs ōrātiōnem fac_____. _____

10. Equī raedam trah_____. _____

    _____

11. Mīles fortiter pugn_____. _____

    _____

12. Antōnius et soror patrem exspect_____. _____

    _____

PRACTICE FOUR

Complete the Latin translation of the following English verb phrases. The first one is done for you.

1. you (s.) led	<u>dūcēbās</u>		6. I began to turn	<u>vert</u>	
2. he used to advise	<u>mōn</u>		7. we kept on annoying	<u>vex</u>	
3. we were fortifying	<u>mūn</u>		8. I was desiring	<u>cup</u>	
4. they sang	<u>can</u>		9. we kept on searching	<u>pet</u>	
5. it began to fall	<u>cad</u>		10. you (pl.) laughed	<u>rīd</u>	

CHAPTER IV — THE FUTURE TENSE

THE FORMATION OF THE FUTURE TENSE

The future tense of regular verbs is formed from the present stem of the verb. The various verb conjugations use three different sets of tense signs to indicate the future tense. However all, verb conjugations still use the personal endings **-ō(m), -s, -t, -mus, -tis, -nt**. Look below at the summary of how the future tense is formed.

1) First and Second conjugations take a tense sign of **-bi-**. The linking vowel for 1st conjugation is **-ā**, for 2nd conjugation **-ē**. Look at the model verbs below.

I amō, <u>amā</u>re	II doceō, <u>docē</u>re
amābō	docēbō
amābis	docēbis
amābit	docēbit
amābimus	docēbimus
amābitis	docēbitis
amābunt	docēbunt

NOTA BENE:
> In the first person singular, the personal ending **-ō** covers up the **-i** of the tense sign **-bi-**.
> In the third person plural, the tense sign **-bi-** becomes **-bu-**.

2) Third conjugation verbs use the tense sign **one -a** (for 1st person singular) and **five -e's** (for 1st person plural, 2nd person singular and plural, and 3rd person singular and plural).

III regō, <u>rege</u>re
regam
regēs
reget
regēmus
regētis
regent

3) Third io and Fourth conjugation verbs take a tense sign of **one -ia** (for 1st person singular) and **five -ie's** (for 1st person plural, 2nd person singular and plural, and 3rd person singular and plural).

IIIio capiō <u>capere</u>	IV muniō <u>munīre</u>
capiam	muniam
capiēs	muniēs
capiet	muniet
capiēmus	muniēmus
capiētis	muniētis
capient	munient

NOTA BENE:
> The personal ending of the 1st person singular in the future tense of 3rd and 4th conjugation verbs is **-m**, instead of **-ō**.

HOW TO TRANSLATE THE FUTURE TENSE

The future tense is used in Latin to denote an action that has not yet happened. To translate a Latin verb in the Future tense into English you use the helping verb **will.**

> Puella in agrīs **ambulābit.**   *The girl will walk in the fields.*

IS IT PRESENT OR FUTURE?

Be careful, because the linking vowel **-e** can signal two different tenses. This is why it is important to know your verb conjugations. For 2nd conjugation verbs **-e** signals the present tense. For 3rd conjugation verbs **-e** signals the future tense.

> Puella canem vid**e**t. (2nd conj.)   *The girl sees the dog.*
> Puellam canem pet**e**t. (3rd conj.)   *The girl will look for the dog.*

PRACTICE ONE

Complete the future tense conjugation charts for each of the following verbs. Use the model verbs on pages one hundred eleven and one hundred twelve as your guide.

	perveniō, pervenīre	dōnō, dōnāre	timeō, timēre
1st. sing.			
2nd sing.			
3rd. sing.			
1st pl.			
2nd pl.			
3rd pl.			

	cōniciō, cōnicere	cadō, cadere	careō, carēre
1st. sing.			
2nd sing.			
3rd. sing.			
1st pl.			
2nd pl.			
3rd pl.			

PRACTICE TWO

Change each of the following verbs in the present tense to the future tense, keeping the same person and number.

1. descenditis _____

2. manent _____

3. audīmus _____

4. arripis _____

5. portō _____

6. ambulātis _____

7. capiō _____

8. dūcit _____

9. iacis _____

10. pūniunt _____

PRACTICE THREE

Circle the verb that is in the future tense in each of the following pairs of verbs.

1. tenēbis   agēbat

2. terrēs   ducētis

3. audient   regit

4. faciam   capis

5. maneō   spectābit

6. dicēmus   movēs

PRACTICE FOUR

Circle the verb in each of the following sentences and identify whether it is in the present or the future tense. Then translate each sentence into English.

Present or **Future**

1. Ego in urbe multōs diēs manēbō.   _____

_____

2. Meus servus librōs inveniet.   _____

_____

3. Noster dux numquam multōs captīvōs capit.   _____

_____

4. Ille hostēs in pugnā interficit.   _____

_____

5. Nōs pīrātās scelestōs petēmus.   _____

_____

6. Cur tū rīdēs?   _____

_____

7. In tabernā huius macellī bonam carnem emit.   _____

_____

8. Aurīgae magnā curā habēnās equōrum tenent.   _____

_____

CHAPTER V — INFINITIVE AND IMPERATIVE VERB FORMS

· ·

THE PRESENT INFINITIVE

The present infinitive is always the **second form** of a verb that you find when you look up a verb in a Latin dictionary.   For all regular verbs, **the second form** or **the second principal part** ends in **-re.**

spectō, spectā**re**, spectāvī, spectātus	1st conjugation
doceō, docē**re**, docuī, doctus	2nd conjugation
petō, pete**re**, petīvī, petītus	3rd conjugation
capiō, cape**re**, cēpī, captus	3rd io conjugation
audiō, audī**re**, audīvī, audītus	4th conjugation

An infinitive can never be the only verb form in a sentence. The infinitive helps to complete the meaning or action of certain other verbs. The following verbs often use infinitives to complete their meaning or action.

amō, amāre	*to like (to)*
cupiō, cupere	*to desire (to)*
nōlō, nōlle	*to be unwilling (to)*
parō, parāre	*to prepare or get ready (to)*
possum, posse	*to be able (to) or can*
est	*it is*
volō, velle	*to wish (to)*

Puella in agrīs **ambulāre** amat.	*The girl likes **to walk** in the fields.*
Tūne forum hodiē **vidēre** cupis?	*Do you desire **to see** the forum today?*

NOTA BENE:
   The Latin infinitive is translated into English as **to** _____.
   The infinitive ending is always **-re.** Infinitives **do not** agree in person and number with the main verb of the sentence; the ending *never* changes.

PRACTICE ONE

In each sentence circle the infinitive and draw an arrow to the main verb on which it depends. Then translate the sentence into English.

1. Antōnia novam stolam emere cupit.

   _____

2. Mercātōrēs multās stolās vendere volunt.

   _____

3. Mercatōrēs nunc omnēs stolās Antōniae mōnstrāre volunt.

   _____

4. Mater Antōniae dīcit, "Tempus est discēdere!"

   _____

5. Manē milītēs hostem pugnāre parant.

   _____

6. Paucī milītēs pugnāre nōlunt.

   _____

7. Amāsne spectāre gladiātōrēs in arēnā?

   _____

PRACTICE TWO

Circle the correct verb form to complete the sentence. Then translate each sentence into English.

1. Antōnius et amīcī hodiē quaestiōnibus magistrī (respondēre / respondent) possunt.

   _____

2. Antōnius et amīcī hodiē quaestiōnibus magistrī (respondēre / respondent).

   _____

3. Mea fīlia (cantat / cantāre) amat.

   _____

4. Mea fīlia semper (cantat / cantāre).

_____

5. Omnēs servī in culīnā nōn (labōrāre / labōrant).

_____

6. Omnēs servī in culīnā (labōrāre / labōrant) nōn parant.

_____

7. Quod sum dēfessa, hīc (maneō / manēre) volō.

_____

8. Quod sum dēfessa, hīc (maneō / manēre).

_____

9. Canis mē (terret / terrēre).

_____

10. Canis mē (terret / terrēre) potest.

_____

IMPERATIVES

Imperatives are formed from the stem of the second principal part of a verb. Imperative forms are only found in the second person singular or the second person plural. Imperatives are used to give commands in the second person.

Verb Conjugation	Infinitve form	Singular Imperative	Plural Imperative	English Meaning
1st	amāre	Amā	Amāte	_Love!_
2nd	docēre	Docē	Docēte	_Teach!_
3rd	regere	Rege	Regite	_Rule!_
3rd io	capere	Cape	Capite	_Seize!_
4th	mūnīre	Mūnī	Mūnīte	_Fortify!_

NOTA BENE:
   The singular imperative is just the present stem of the verb.
   The plural imperative is the present stem plus **-te**.
   Except in the 3rd conjugation a weak **-e** turns to **-i** when followed by a consonant. Hence reg**e** and cap**e**, but reg**i**te and cap**i**te.
   Dūc, dīc, and **fac** are irregular imperative forms. However their plurals are regular: **dūcite, dīcite,** and **facite.**

Negative commands are formed using **nōlī** (singular) and **nōlīte** (plural) plus the infinitive of the verb.

Infinitive form	Singular Imperative	Plural Imperative	English Meaning
amāre	Nōlī amāre	Nōlīte amāre	*Don't love!*
docēre	Nōlī docēre	Nōlīte docēre	*Don't teach!*
regere	Nōlī regere	Nōlīte regere	*Don't rule!*
capere	Nōlī capere	Nōlīte capere	*Don't seize!*
mūnīre	Nōlī mūnīre	Nōlīte mūnīre	*Don't fortify!*

PRACTICE THREE

On a separate sheet of paper give the positive and negative imperatives of each of the following verbs.

1. surgō, surgere
2. habeō, habēre
3. iaceō, iacēre
4. dīcō, dīcere
5. sentiō, sentīre
6. laudō, laudāre
7. temptō, temptāre
8. incipiō, incipere
9. dūcō, dūcere

PRACTICE FOUR

Identify each verb form as being present tense or an imperative. Change the Latin forms from singular to plural or plural to singular. Finally, translate the new Latin forms into English. The first one is done for you.

1. facite!   Imper.   Fac   Make (sing.)
2. agit   _____   _____   _____
3. nōlī invenīre   _____   _____   _____
4. maneō   _____   _____   _____
5. ōrāte   _____   _____   _____
6. petitis   _____   _____   _____
7. nōlīte cantāre   _____   _____   _____
8. dūc   _____   _____   _____
9. pervenis   _____   _____   _____
10. docent   _____   _____   _____

PRACTICE FIVE

Write the Latin commands that would result in the following actions. Make all necessary changes. The first one is done for you.

1. Servus cistās dominī parat. <u>Serve, cistās dominī parā!</u>

2. Puerī in villā nōn currunt. _____

3. Uxōrēs domum celeriter festīnant. _____

4. Senātor longam ōrātiōnem facit. _____

5. Pater servōs ad villam nōn mittit. _____

6. Antōnius matrī respondet. _____

7. Claudia et Antōnia epistulās scrībunt. _____

CHAPTER VI — THE PRESENT SYSTEM OF *ESSE, POSSE, FERRE, IRE, VELLE,* AND *NOLLE*

· ·

IRREGULAR VERBS

Irregular verbs do not form their present, impefect and future tenses in a consistent manner. Also note that most of the verbs have infinitives that do not end in **-re.**

THE PRESENT TENSE

It is in the present tense that these verbs have the most irregular patterns. These forms need to be memorized.

sum, esse	possum, posse	volō, velle	nōlō, nōlle	ferō, ferre	eō, īre
sum	possum	volō	nōlō	fero	eō
es	potes	vīs	nōn vīs	fers	īs
est	potest	vult	nōn vult	fert	it
sumus	possumus	volumus	nōlumus	ferimus	īmus
estis	potestis	vultis	nōn vultis	fertis	ītis
sunt	possunt	volunt	nōlunt	ferunt	eunt

NOTA BENE:
> Remember that **posse** is a compound of the verb **esse.** To form the verb forms of **posse** you place **pos-** in front of any form of **esse** that begins with **s** (**s**um, **pos**sum) and **pot-** in front of any form of **esse** that begins with **e** (**e**st, **pot**est).

THE IMPERFECT TENSE

For the imperfect tense the patterns of the irregular verbs are more predictable.

sum, esse	possum, posse	volō, velle	nōlō, nōlle	ferō, ferre	eō, īre
eram	poteram	volēbam	nōlēbam	ferēbam	ībam
erās	poterās	volēbās	nōlēbās	ferēbās	ībās
erat	poterat	volēbat	nōlēbat	ferēbat	ībat
erāmus	poterāmus	volēbāmus	nōlēbāmus	ferēbāmus	ībāmus
erātis	poterātis	volēbātis	nōlēbātis	ferēbātis	ībātis
erant	poterant	volēbant	nōlēbant	ferēbant	ībant

NOTA BENE:
> Except for **esse** and **posse,** the tense sign of the imperfect tense is still **-bā-.**
> The tense sign of the imperfect tenses of **esse** and **posse** is **erā-.**

THE FUTURE TENSE

For the future tense the patterns of the irregular verbs can be placed into three categories.

1) **Esse** and **posse** take **eri-** as their tense sign for the future, except in the first person singular and the third person plural.

2) **Velle, nōlle,** and **ferre** here act like 3rd conjugation verbs (and take **one a** and **five e's** for their Future tense sign).

3) **Īre** here acts in a way as if it belonged to the 1st or 2nd conjugation. It takes **-bi-** for its future tense sign.

sum, esse	possum, posse	volō, velle	nōlō, nōlle	ferō, ferre	eō, īre
erō	poterō	volam	nōlam	feram	ībō
eris	poteris	volēs	nōlēs	ferēs	ībis
erit	poterit	volet	nōlet	feret	ībit
erimus	poterimus	volēmus	nōlēmus	ferēmus	ībimus
eritis	poteritis	volētis	nōlētis	ferētis	ībitis
erunt	poterunt	volent	nōlent	ferent	ībunt

IMPERATIVE OF IRREGULAR VERBS

The following irregular verbs have imperative verb forms.

Infinitive form	Singular Imperative	Plural Imperative
esse	es	este
nōlle	nōlī	nōlīte
ferre	fer	ferte
īre	ī	īte

PRACTICE ONE

Complete the verb charts for the following irregular verbs. Use the verb models on pages one hundred twenty and one hundred twenty one as your guide. The first one is done for you.

	Present	Imperfect	Future
1.	fers	ferēbās	ferēs
2.		ībant	
3.	possumus		
4.		nōlēbat	
5.	sum		
6.			volētis

PRACTICE TWO

Translate each of the following irregular verb forms into English.

1. it _____
2. nōlle _____
3. poteritis _____
4. eunt _____
5. ī _____
6. nōlam _____
7. ībō _____
8. erāmus _____
9. poterant _____
10. nōlīte ferre _____

11. ferēbant _____
12. posse _____
13. volēmus _____
14. erō _____
15. vult _____
16. sumus _____
17. feret _____
18. volēbātis _____
19. īre _____
20. este _____

PRACTICE THREE

Translate the following English verb forms into Latin.

a. **sum, esse**

1. I will be _____

2. You were _____

3. to be _____

4. He is _____

5. I used to be _____

6. Be! (s.) _____

b. **ferō, ferre**

1. Bring! (pl.) _____

2. They will bring _____

3. Don't bring (s.) _____

4. to bring _____

5. He brought _____

6. We do bring _____

c. **eō, īre**

1. I began to go _____

2. to go _____

3. We will go _____

4. Don't go! (s.) _____

5. Go! (s.) _____

6. She is going _____

d. **volō, velle**

1. to wish _____

2. I do wish _____

3. They wished _____

4. You (s.) wish _____

5. I will wish _____

6. We wish _____

PRACTICE FOUR

Circle the irregular verb in each sentence. Identify the verb as present, imperfect, future or imperative. Then translate the sentence into English. Watch your verb tenses.

Verb Form

1. Paedagōgus cum puerīs ad lūdum it.   _____

   _____

2. Paedagōgus cum puerīs ad lūdum ībat.   _____

   _____

3. Paedagōgus cum puerīs ad lūdum ībit.   _____

   _____

4. Paedagōge, cum puerīs ad lūdum ī!   _____

   _____

5. Mea uxor ad Circum ambulāre nōn vult.   _____

   _____

6. Mea uxor ad Circum ambulāre nōlet.   _____

   _____

7. Mea uxor, nōlī ambulāre ad Circum!   _____

   _____

8. Mea uxor ad Circum ambulāre nōlēbat.   _____

   _____

9. Pater, cur novum coquum invenīre nōn poterās?   _____

   _____

10. Pater, cur novum coquum invenīre nōn poteris?   _____

    _____

11. Pater, cur novum coquum invenīre nōn potes?   _____

    _____

CHAPTER VII — REVIEW OF THE PRESENT SYSTEM ACTIVE

. . . .

SUMMARY OF THE PRESENT SYSTEM ACTIVE

PRESENT TENSE

Present Stem + Personal endings:

I	II	III	IIIio	IV
amō, <u>amā</u>re	doceō, <u>docē</u>re	regō, <u>rege</u>re	capiō, <u>cape</u>re	mūniō, <u>mūnī</u>re
amō	doceō	regō	capiō	mūniō
amās	docēs	regis	capis	mūnīs
amat, etc.	docet, etc.	regit, etc.	capit , etc.	mūnit, etc.

English Translation: I _____, I do _____, I am _____ ing

IMPERFECT TENSE

Present Stem + bā + Personal endings:

I	II	III	IIIio	IV
amō, <u>amā</u>re	doceō, <u>docē</u>re	regō, <u>rege</u>re	capiō, <u>cape</u>re	muniō, <u>munī</u>re
amābam	docēbam	regēbam	capiēbam	muniēbam
amābās	docēbās	regēbās	capiēbās	muniēbās
amābat , etc.	docēbat, etc.	regēbat, etc.	capiēbat, etc.	muniēbat , etc.

English Translation: I_____ed, I was _____ing, I kept on _____ing,

                              I used to _____, I began to _____

FUTURE TENSE

Present Stem + bi+ Personal endings for 1st & 2nd conjugations

Present Stem + 1 a and 5 e's + Personal endings for 3rd conjugation

Present Stem + 1 ia and 5 ie's + Personal endings for 3rd io & 4th conjugations

I	II	III	IIIio	IV
amō, <u>amā</u>re	doceō, <u>docē</u>re	regō, <u>rege</u>re	capiō, <u>cape</u>re	muniō, <u>munī</u>re
amābō	docēbō	regam	capiam	muniam
amābis	docēbis	regēs	capiēs	muniēs
amābit , etc.	docēbit, etc.	reget, etc.	capiet, etc.	muniet, etc.

English Translation: I will _____

PRACTICE ONE

*Identify the one verb that is **not** in the same number as the other verbs. Place the letter of your answer in the blanks provided.*

____1. a. habētis   b. agō   c. tenēbam   d. fac

____2. a. sunt   b. movēbātis   c. lacrimās   d. gerēmus

____3. a. nōlīte cantāre b. audiēbātis   c. poterant   d. veniam

____4. a. sedeō   b. fert   c. capite   d. clamābis

____5. a. incipiō   b. vidēmus   c. volunt   d. dūcitis

PRACTICE TWO

*Identify the one verb that is **not** in the same tense or mood as the other verbs. Place the letter of your answer in the blanks provided.*

____1. a. erāmus   b. volēbam   c. spectābat   d. manēte

____2. a. dōnābit   b. poterimus   c. efficiam   d. pūniēbat

____3. a. īte   b. finīte   c. valēre   d. carpe

____4. a. induet   b. terrēs   c. nōn vult   d. possunt

____5. a. nōlle   b. nōlīte īre   c. ridēre   d. pervenīre

PRACTICE THREE

Select the correct English translation for each of the following Latin verbs. Place the letter of your answer in the blanks provided.

____1. voluimus   a. we wished   b. we were wishing   c. we will wish

____2. pōnent   a. they place   b. they will place   c. they placed

____3. teneō   a. I do hold   b. I will hold   c. I used to hold

____4. pervenītis   a. you arrived   b. you will arrive   c. you are arriving

____5. lacrimāre   a. to cry   b. Cry!   c. I cried

____6. poterās   a. you will be able   b. you were able   c. you are able

____7. Nōlī currere   a. to run   b. you ran   c. Don't run!

____8. ambulābant   a. they will walk   b. they used to walk   c. they do walk

____9. clamābō   a. I will shout   b. I began to shout   c. I am shouting

___10. īte   a. to go   b. you were going   c. Go!

PRACTICE FOUR

Write the name of the form, each of which uses the present active stem, in the blanks provided. Forms may be found in the present, imperfect, or future tense or as an imperative or infinitive. Then translate the forms into English. The first one is done for you.

	Form	English Translation
1. portābō	future	I will carry
2. timēmus	_____	_____
3. eram	_____	_____
4. mutābās	_____	_____
5. pōnētis	_____	_____
6. carēbunt	_____	_____
7. volēbam	_____	_____
8. ī	_____	_____
9. finīre	_____	_____
10. audiunt	_____	_____

(cont.)

11. dūcit   _____   _____

12. nōlī sedēre   _____   _____

13. capiēbat   _____   _____

14. fer   _____   _____

15. parāte   _____   _____

16. cupiam   _____   _____

17. demōnstrō   _____   _____

18. mittitis   _____   _____

19. poteris   _____   _____

20. nōn vīs   _____   _____

PRACTICE FIVE

Read through the passage below and answer the questions which follow <u>in English</u>.

Aeneas Says Goodbye to Dido

Regīna, necesse est mihi tuam urbem relinquere. Deī mē ad Ītaliam īre iubent. Etiam Gryneus Apollō et Lyciae sortēs mē īre cupiunt. Meus pater Anchīsēs in somniō mē monēbat. Nūntium Iovis ipsīus vidēbam et eius vōcem hīs auribus audiēbam. Nunc, Elissa, nōlīte clāmāre! Numquam tuum marītum esse prōmittēbam. Sed semper tē in memoriā tenēbō. Ad Ītaliam meā sponte nōn eō.   5

Gryneus, -a, -um	*of Gryneus*	**ipse, ipsa, ipsum**	*himself, herself*
Lycia, -ae, f.	*country of Asia*		*itself*
	Minor	**Elissa, -ae, f.**	*Dido*
sors, sortis, f.	*oracle*	**spōns, spontis, f.**	*wish, will*

1. Who orders Aeneas to Italy?_____

2. How does Anchises warn his son?_____

3. Whose voice has Aeneas heard?_____

4. Will Aeneas ever forget Dido?_____

PRACTICE SIX

From the story "Aeneas Says Goodby to Dido" give examples of the following verb forms:

Present Tense	Future Tense	Imperative
1. _____	1. _____	1. _____
2. _____		

Infinitive	Imperfect Tense
1. _____	1. _____
2. _____	2. _____
3. _____	3. _____

PRACTICE SEVEN

From the pool of verb forms below select the Latin verb forms that properly complete the following sentences. You will not use all the verb forms given.

Dido's Reply to Aeneas

Tēne nihil movet? Diū dolōrōsa eram, _____ *(I was crying)* quod tē _____

(to stay) volēbam. Mandātō deōrum ad Ītaliam _____ *(you are going).* Sīc tū

_____ *(say).* Tibi nōn crēdō. Sed perfide, _____ *(go)!* _____ *(Seek)*

Ītaliam! Ego hīc tē tenēre _____ *(do not wish).* Sed ūnō diē, deī tibi poenās dabunt.

Meum nōmen _____ *(you will call)* et audiam. Tua fāma ad mē, quae erit in   5

regiōne Plutōnis, _____ *(will come).*

perfidus, -a, -um   *wicked, treacherous*   **fāma, -ae, f.**   *reputation*

lacrimābam	nōlō	dīc	ī
lacrimābō	nolle	venit	nōlī petere
vocāte	manēbat	veniet	pete
vocābis	manēre	is	dīcis

PRACTICE EIGHT

In the space provided below, write out an English translation of the story "Dido's Reply to Aeneas".

_____

_____

_____

_____

_____

_____

_____

_____

_____

_____

CHAPTER VIII — THE PERFECT TENSE
. . . .

THE FORMATION OF THE PERFECT TENSE

The perfect tense of **both** regular and irregular verbs is formed by adding the special perfect personal verb endings *-ī, -istī, -it, -imus, -istis, -ērunt* to the **stem** of the **3rd principal part** of any Latin verb. Look at the charts below:

Personal Verb Endings for the Perfect Tense Active					
Singular			*Plural*		
English Pronoun	Latin Verb Ending	Latin Pronoun	English Pronoun	Latin Verb Ending	Latin Pronoun
I	**-ī**	Ego	*We*	**-imus**	Nōs
You	**-istī**	Tū	*You*	**-istis**	Vōs
He, She, It	**-it**	Is, Ea, Id	*They*	**-ērunt**	Eī, Eae, Ea

I	II	III	IIIio	IV
amō, amāre, amāvī	doceō, docēre, docuī	regō, regere, rēxī	capiō, capere, cēpī	mūniō, mūnīre, mūnīvī
amāvī	docuī	rēxī	cēpī	mūnīvī
amāvistī	docuistī	rēxistī	cēpistī	mūnīvistī
amāvit	docuit	rēxit	cēpit	mūnīvit
amāvimus	docuimus	rēximus	cēpimus	mūnīvimus
amāvistis	docuistis	rēxistis	cēpistis	mūnīvistis
amāvērunt	docuērunt	rēxērunt	cēpērunt	munīvērunt

IRREGULAR VERBS

sum, esse fuī	possum, posse potuī	volō, velle voluī	nōlō, nōlle nōluī	ferō, ferre tulī	eō, īre īvī
fuī	potuī	voluī	nōluī	tulī	īvī
fuistī	potuistī	voluistī	nōluistī	tulistī	īvistī
fuit	potuit	voluit	nōluit	tulit	īvit
fuimus	potuimus	voluimus	nōluimus	tulimus	īvimus
fuistis	potuistis	voluistis	nōluistis	tulistis	īvistis
fuērunt	potuērunt	voluērunt	nōluērunt	tulērunt	īvērunt

HOW TO IDENTIFY THE PERFECT STEM

You can always identify or recognize the perfect stem because of its unique **stem markers**. The perfect stems of all Latin verbs always end in **-s, -u, -v, -x,** or a **vowel change**. Look at the examples below.

Principal Parts	Present Tense	Perfect Tense	Stem Marker
amō, amāre, amāvī	amat	amāvit	-v
doceō, docēre, docuī	docet	docuit	-u
regō, regere, rēxī	regit	rēxit	-x
mittō, mittere, mīsī	mittit	mīsit	-s
capiō, capere, cēpī	capit	cēpit	vowel change
veniō, venīre, vēnī	venit	vēnit	vowel change

NOTA BENE:
Most 1st and 4th conjugation verbs have a **-v** stem marker.
Most 2nd conjugation verbs have a **-u** stem marker.
The irregular verb **ferō, ferre, tulī, lātus** does not follow the regular pattern for stem markers.

HOW TO TRANSLATE THE PERFECT TENSE

The perfect tense is used in Latin to denote a **completed** action that has occurred in the past. There are several ways to translate the Latin perfect tense into English. Once again it is up to you to decide which is the best English translation by looking at the context of the sentence within the paragraph or story.

Puella in agrīs **ambulāvit.**

*The girl **walked** in the fields (and is walking no longer).*

*The girl **did walk** in the fields.*

*The girl **has walked** in the fields.*

NOTA BENE:
Note that Latin does not use any helping verbs in the perfect tense.

PRACTICE ONE

Circle the perfect stem for each verb. Then complete the perfect tense conjugation charts for each of the following verbs. Use the model verbs on page one hundred thirty one as your guide.

	faciō, facere, fēcī	videō, vidēre, vīdī	cantō, cantāre, cantāvī
1st. sing.			
2nd sing.			
3rd. sing.			
1st pl.			
2nd pl.			
3rd pl.			

	possum, posse, potuī	dūcō, dūcere, dūxī	sentiō, sentīre, sēnsī
1st. sing.			
2nd sing.			
3rd. sing.			
1st pl.			
2nd pl.			
3rd pl.			

PRACTICE TWO

Circle the perfect stem marker and underline the perfect personal verb ending for each of the following verbs. Then from the pool of nouns and pronouns select the correct one to agree with the verb form and write it in the blank provided. You may use an answer more than once.

_____1. ēgit

_____2. admīsistis

_____3. mānsī

_____4. nōluimus

_____5. dormīvērunt

_____6. stetit

_____7. iēcī

_____8. tenuistī

_____9. tulimus

Ego	Tū	Puella
Nōs	Vōs	Puellae

PRACTICE THREE

Underline the stem of the verb in each of the following sentences and identify whether it is in the present tense or perfect tense. Then translate each sentence into English.

Present or **Perfect**

1. Nunc rēx in Ītaliā nōn regit. _____

   _____

2. Multōs annōs rēx in Ītaliā nōn rēxit. _____

   _____

3. Herī novum consilium cēpimus. _____

   _____

4. Hodiē novum consilium capimus. _____

   _____

5. Paedagōgus puerōs ad lūdum dūcit. _____

   _____

6. Paedagōgus puerōs ad lūdum dūxit. _____

   _____

7. Dominus scelestōs servōs pūnīvit. _____

   _____

8. Dominus scelestōs servōs pūnit. _____

   _____

9. Multī milītēs in Campō Martiō sunt. _____

   _____

10. Multī milītēs in Campō Martiō fuērunt. _____

    _____

11. Quis in hāc insulā habitāvit? _____

    _____

12. Quis in hāc insulā habitat? _____

    _____

PRACTICE FOUR

Change the following verbs in the present tense to the perfect tense, keeping the same person and number.

1. dīcunt   _____

2. habēmus   _____

3. rīdeō   _____

4. pugnātis   _____

5. fers   _____

6. nōn vult   _____

7. advenis   _____

8. labōrō   _____

9. audītis   _____

10. agimus   _____

THE IMPERFECT TENSE VERSUS THE PERFECT TENSE

Both the imperfect and perfect tenses are used to denote actions that have happened in the past. The imperfect tense denotes a repeated or incompleted action in the past. The perfect tense denotes a one-time or completed action in the past. Look at the examples below.

Imperfect
    Diū puella in agrīs **ambulābat**.   *For a long time the girl **was walking** in the fields.*

Perfect
    Herī puella in agrīs **ambulāvit**.   *Yesterday the girl **walked** in the fields.*

Imperfect
    Puella in agrīs **ambulābat**.   *The girl **began to walk** in the fields.*

Perfect
    Puella in agrīs **ambulāvit**.   *The girl **did walk** in the fields.*

Imperfect
    Puella in agrīs **ambulābat**.   *The girl **used to walk** in the fields.*

Perfect
    Puella in agrīs **ambulāvit**.   *The girl **has walked** in the fields.*

PRACTICE FIVE

Read through the story below and answer <u>in English</u> the questions that follow.

In this passage Aeneas is relating to Dido and the other banquet guests how after the fall of Troy he searched for his lost wife Creusa.

Aeneas Searches for Creusa

Ego cum patre et fīliō Trōiā fugiēbam. Mea uxor Creūsa ā tergō ambulābat. Respēxī et mea uxor in hōc locō nōn iam erat. Ubi erat mea uxor? Nunc eram similis virō īnsānō. Ad urbem revēnī. Meam Creūsam petēbam. Maestus iterum et iterum eius nōmen vocābam. Sed in nūllō locō meam uxōrem vīdī.

Subitō ante meōs oculōs imāginem meae Creūsae vīdī. Obstipuī, stetēruntque meae   5
comae. Diū dīcere nōn poteram.

Deinde mea uxor haec verba mihi dīxit: "O dulcis coniūnx, nōlī indulgēre tuō īnsānō dolōrī. Nōn sine nūmine deōrum haec ēvēnērunt. Tibi longa exsilia erunt. Post multōs annōs ad Hesperiam veniēs. Ibi novum regnum et novam uxōrem habēbis. Ego sum laeta. Ego ad Graeciam nōn ībō. Ego serva Graeca nōn erō. Necesse est mihi hīc manēre.   10
Magna genetrīx deōrum in hōc locō mē dētinuit. Nunc valē! Et servā amōrem commūnis fīliī."

Ubi haec verba dīxit, mea uxor in aurās recessit. Ter collō dāre bracchia circum temptābam. Ter eius umbra manūs effūgit. Dēmum ad patrem et fīlium sociōsque redīvī.   15

Trōiā	*from Troy*	**aura, -ae, f.**	*breeze*
maestus, -a, -um	*sad*	**ter** (adv.)	*three times*
imāgō, imāginis, f.	*image, ghost*	**collō dāre bracchia**	*to put my arms*
nūmen, nūminis, n.	*divine will*	**circum**	*around her neck*
exsilium, -ī, n.	*exile*	**dēmum**	*at last, finally*
genetrīx, genetrīcis, f.	*mother*		

obstipēscō, obstipēscere, obstipuī	*to be dazed*
stō, stāre, stetī, status	*to stand*
indulgeō, indulgēre, indulsī, indultus	*to indulge*
(+ dative)	
ēveniō, ēvenīre, ēvēnī, ēventus	*to happen, turn out*
recēdō, recēdere, recessī, recessus	*to depart, to retire*

1. At the start of this passage who is with Aeneas?_____

_____

2. How does Aeneas react when he discovers that his wife has disappeared?_____

_____

3. What happens to Aeneas when he first sees his wife again?_____

_____

4. What knowledge of the future does Creusa give to Aeneas?_____

_____

5. Why is Creusa happy?_____

_____

PRACTIE SIX

From the story on the preceding page, list in the appropriate columns all the verbs in the imperfect and perfect tenses, the line number, and a suitable English translation of each verb form. The first one for each tense is done for you.

	Imperfect Tense Verbs	Line #	English Translation
1.	fugiēbam	1	I was fleeing
2.			
3.			
4.			
5.			
6.			
7.			
8.			
9.			

	Perfect Tense Verbs	Line #	English Translation
1.	Respēxī	1	I looked back
2.			
3.			
4.			
5.			
6.			
7.			
8.			
9.			
10.			
11.			
12.			
13.			

Chapter IX — The Pluperfect and Future Perfect Tenses

· ·

THE FORMATION OF THE PLUPERFECT AND FUTURE PERFECT TENSES

The pluperfect tense of **both** regular and irregular verbs is formed by adding the tense sign **-erā-** and the regular personal verb endings *-m, -s -t, -mus, -tis, -nt* to the **stem** of the **3rd principal part** of any Latin verb. Look at the charts below: the perfect stem is underlined for you.

THE PLUPERFECT TENSE

I amō, amāre, <u>amāvī</u>	II doceō, docēre, <u>docuī</u>	III regō, regere, <u>rēxī</u>	IIIio capiō, capere, <u>cēpī</u>	IV mūniō, mūnīre, <u>mūnīvī</u>
amāveram	docueram	rēxeram	cēperam	mūnīveram
amāverās	docuerās	rēxerās	cēperās	mūnīverās
amāverat	docuerat	rēxerat	cēperat	mūnīverat
amāverāmus	docuerāmus	rēxerāmus	cēperāmus	mūnīverāmus
amāverātis	docuerātis	rēxerātis	cēperātis	mūnīverātis
amāverant	docuerant	rēxerant	cēperant	mūnīverant

IRREGULAR VERBS

sum, esse, <u>fuī</u>	possum, posse, <u>potuī</u>	volō, velle, <u>voluī</u>	nōlō, nōlle, <u>nōluī</u>	ferō, ferre, <u>tulī</u>	eō, īre, <u>īvī</u>
<u>fu</u>eram	<u>potu</u>eram	<u>volu</u>eram	<u>nōlu</u>eram	<u>tul</u>eram	<u>īv</u>eram
<u>fu</u>erās	<u>potu</u>erās	<u>volu</u>erās	<u>nōlu</u>erās	<u>tul</u>erās	<u>īv</u>erās
<u>fu</u>erat, etc.	<u>potu</u>erat, etc.	<u>volu</u>erat, etc.	<u>nōlu</u>erat, etc.	<u>tul</u>erat, etc.	<u>īv</u>erat, etc.

THE FUTURE PERFECT TENSE

The future perfect tense of **both** regular and irregular verbs is formed by adding the tense sign **-eri-** and the personal verb endings *-ō, -s, -t, -mus, -tis, -nt* to the **stem** of the **3rd principal part** of any Latin verb. Look at the charts below: The perfect stem is underlined for you.

I	II	III	IIIio	IV
amō, amāre, amāvī	doceō, docēre, docuī	regō, regere, rēxī	capiō, capere, cēpī	mūniō, mūnīre, mūnīvī
amāverō	docuerō	rēxerō	cēperō	mūnīverō
amāveris	docueris	rēxeris	cēperis	mūnīveris
amāverit	docuerit	rēxerit	cēperit	mūnīverit
amāverimus	docuerimus	rēxerimus	cēperimus	mūnīverimus
amāveritis	docueritis	rēxeritis	cēperitis	mūnīveritis
amāverint	docuerint	rēxerint	cēperint	mūnīverint

IRREGULAR VERBS

sum, esse, fuī	possum, posse, potuī	volō, velle, voluī	nōlo, nōlle, nōluī	ferō, ferre, tulī	eō, īre, īvī
fuerō	potuerō	voluerō	nōluerō	tulerō	īverō
fueris	potueris	volueris	nōlueris	tuleris	īveris
fuerit, etc.	potuerit, etc.	voluerit, etc.	nōluerit, etc.	tulerit, etc.	īverit, etc.

HOW TO TRANSLATE THE PLUPERFECT AND FUTURE PERFECT TENSES

The pluperfect tense is used in Latin to denote an action that has occurred farther back in the past than the perfect tense.

Abhinc multōs annōs fēmina, ut puella, in hīs agrīs **ambulāverat.**

*Many years ago the woman, as a girl, **had walked in these fields.***

The future perfect tense is used in Latin to denote an action that will have occurred or been completed by some specific time in the future.

Crās puella in hīs agrīs **ambulāverit.**   *By tomorrow the girl **will have walked in these fields.***

NOTA BENE:
Note that Latin does not use any helping verbs in the pluperfect or future perfect tenses.

PRACTICE ONE

Keeping the same person and number, change each of the following verbs in the perfect tense to the pluperfect and future perfect tenses. Use the verb models on pages 138-139 as your guide.

Perfect	Pluperfect	Future Perfect
1. ēgimus	_____	_____
2. fuit	_____	_____
3. respēxērunt	_____	_____
4. tulī	_____	_____
5. laudāvistis	_____	_____
6. finīvistī	_____	_____
7. nōluērunt	_____	_____
8. dīxit	_____	_____
9. legimus	_____	_____
10. tenuistī	_____	_____

PRACTICE TWO

Identify the tense of the bold-faced verb in each sentence as perfect, pluperfect, or future perfect. Then translate each sentence into English.

Verb Tense

1. Imperātōr mīlitibus dīxit, "Crās, hostēs **vīcerimus!**"   _____

_____

2. Imperātōrne cum mīlitibus hostēs **vīcit?**   _____

_____

3. Nūntius senatōribus dīxit, "Celeriter imperātōr hostēs **vīcerat.**"   _____

_____

4. Multōs annōs aurīga magnā arte currum **ēgerat.**   _____

_____

5. Sed nunc celerēs equī aurīgam infēlīcem **interfēcit**.

6. Mānē dominus fugitīvum servum nōn **invēnerat**.

7. In quō locō fugitīvus sē **cēlāverit**?

8. Dominus eum in vīcīnam silvam cēlantem **invēnit**.

PRACTICE THREE

Using the four verbs below, translate the following English verb forms into Latin.

pūniō, pūnīre, pūnīvī, pūnītus   *to punish*
doceō, docēre, docuī, doctus   *to teach*
eō, īre, īvī, ītus   *to go*
volō, velle, voluī   *to wish*

1. I did go

2. We had taught

3. You (s.) had punished

4. You (pl.) have taught

5. I wished

6. I will have wished

7. We will have gone

8. They have punished

9. She had gone

10. He will have taught

11. I had wished

12. They will have punished

CHAPTER X — REVIEW OF ALL TENSES OF THE INDICATIVE ACTIVE

. . . .

SUMMARY OF VERB TENSES INDICATIVE ACTIVE

PERSONAL ENDINGS

Personal Endings				Special Endings of the Perfect Tense			
I	-ō (m)	*We*	-mus	*I*	-ī	*We*	-imus
You	-s	*You (pl)*	-tis	*You*	-istī	*You (pl)*	-istis
He, She, It	-t	*They*	-nt	*He, She, It*	-it	*They*	-ērunt

PRESENT TENSE

Present Stem + Personal verb endings:

I	II	III	IIIio	IV
amō, amāre, amāvī	doceō, docēre, docuī	regō, regere, rēxī	capiō, capere, cēpī	mūniō, mūnīre, mūnīvī
amō	doceō	regō	capiō	mūniō
amās	docēs	regis	capis	mūnis
amat etc.	docet, etc.	regit, etc.	capit, etc.	mūnit, etc.

Translation: I _____, I do _____, I am _____ing

IMPERFECT TENSE

Present Stem + bā + Personal verb endings:

I	II	III	IIIio	IV
amō, amāre, amāvī	doceō, docēre, docuī	regō, regere, rēxī	capiō, capere, cēpī	mūniō, mūnīre, mūnīvī
amābam	docēbam	regēbam	capiēbam	mūniēbam
amābās	docēbās	regēbās	capiēbās	mūniēbās
amābat, etc.	docēbat, etc.	regēbat, etc.	capiēbat, etc.	mūniēbat, etc.

Translation: I _____ ed, I was _____ing, I kept on _____ing,
 I used to _____, I began to_____

FUTURE TENSE

Present Stem + bo, bi, bu's + Personal verb endings for 1st & 2nd conjugations

Present Stem + 1 a and 5 e's + Personal verb endings for 3rd conjugation

Present Stem + 1 ia and 5 ie's + Personal verb endings for 3rd io & 4th conjugations

I	II	III	IIIio	IV
amō, amāre, amāvī	doceō, docēre, docuī	regō, regere, rēxī	capiō, capere, cēpī	mūniō, mūnīre, mūnīvī
amābō	docēbō	regam	capiam	mūniam
amābis	docēbis	regēs	capiēs	mūniēs
amābit, etc.	docēbit, etc.	reget, etc.	capiet, etc.	mūniet, etc.

Translation: I will _____

PERFECT TENSE

3rd principal part stem + Special Perfect Personal verb endings:

I	II	III	IIIio	IV
amō, amāre, amāvī	doceō, docēre, docuī	regō, regere, rēxī	capiō, capere, cēpī	mūniō, mūnīre, mūnīvī
amāvī	docuī	rēxī	cēpī	mūnīvī
amāvistī	docuistī	rēxistī	cēpistī	mūnīvistī
amāvit, etc.	docuit, etc.	rēxit, etc.	cēpit, etc.	mūnīvit, etc.

Translation: I _____ed, I did _____, I have _____ed

PLUPERFECT TENSE

3rd principal part stem + erā tense sign + Personal verb endings:

I	II	III	IIIio	IV
amō, amāre, amāvī	doceō, docēre, docuī	regō, regere, rēxī	capiō, capere, cēpī	mūniō, mūnīre, mūnīvī
amāveram	docueram	rēxeram	cēperam	mūnīveram
amāverās	docuerās	rēxerās	cēperās	mūnīverās
amāverat, etc.	docuerat, etc.	rēxerat, etc.	cēperat, etc.	mūnīverat, etc.

Translation: I had_____ed

FUTURE PERFECT TENSE

3rd principal part stem + eri + Personal verb endings:

I	II	III	IIIio	IV
amō, amāre, amāvī	doceō, docēre, docuī	regō, regere, rēxī	capiō, capere, cēpī	mūniō, mūnīre, mūnīvī
amāverō	docuerō	rēxerō	cēperō	mūnīverō
amāveris	docueris	rēxeris	cēperis	mūnīveris
amāverit, etc.	docuerit, etc.	rēxerit, etc.	cēperit, etc.	mūnīverit, etc.

Translation: I will have _____ed

IMPERATIVES

For Positive Commands - the present stem (singular) or the present stem + te (plural)

Verb Conjugation	Infinitive form	Singular Imperative	Plural Imperative	English Meaning
1st	amāre	Amā!	Amāte!	*Love!*
2nd	docēre	Docē!	Docēte!	*Teach!*
3rd	regere	Rege!	Regite!	*Rule!*
3rd io	capere	Cape!	Capite!	*Seize!*
4th	mūnīre	Mūnī!	Mūnīte!	*Fortify!*

Negative Commands - use **nōlī** (singular) and **nōlīte** (plural) plus the infinitive of the verb.

Infinitive form	Singular Imperative	Plural Imperative	English Meaning
amāre	Nōlī amāre!	Nōlīte amāre!	*Don't love!*
docēre	Nōlī docēre!	Nōlīte docēre!	*Don't teach!*
regere	Nōlī regere!	Nōlīte regere!	*Don't rule!*
capere	Nōlī capere!	Nōlīte capere!	*Don't seize!*
mūnīre	Nōlī mūnīre!	Nōlīte mūnīre!	*Don't fortify!*

IRREGULAR VERBS

For the present, imperfect and future tenses of irregular verbs see the charts on pages one hundred twenty and one hundred twenty-one. Remember that the perfect, pluperfect, and future perfect tenses of irregular verbs are formed in the same manner as regular verbs.

PRACTICE ONE

Underline the stems of the following verb forms and then match these forms with their meanings. Use stems to help identify tenses! You will not use all your answers.

agō, agere, ēgī, *to drive*

_____1. agite

_____2. ēgit

_____3. agere

_____4. ēgerit

_____5. agēbat

_____6. agit

a. to drive

b. He does drive

c. Drive!

d. He did drive

e. He will have driven

f. He used to drive

g. He will drive

teneō, tenēre, tenuī, *to hold*

_____1. tenuī

_____2. teneō

_____3. tenēbō

_____4. tenueram

_____5. tenēbam

_____6. tenē

a. I will hold

b. I kept on holding

c. Hold!

d. I have held

e. I am holding

f. to hold

g. I had held

sum, esse, fuī, *to be*

_____1. sunt

_____2. erant

_____3. fuērunt

_____4. esse

_____5. fuerint

_____6. erunt

a. to be

b. They were

c. They will be

d. Be!

e. They will have been

f. They have been

g. They are

PRACTICE TWO

Select the one verb that is **not** in the same tense as the other verbs. Place the letter of your answer in the blanks provided.

_____1. a. erātis   b. potuī   c. faciēbam   d. incipiēbās

_____2. a. eunt   b. aget   c. fers   d. nōn vis

_____3. a. manēs   b. dīcētis   c. poterimus   d. vidēbit

_____4. a. poterit   b. volam   c. spectābant   d. ībimus

_____5. a. clamāvērunt b. tulerō   c. mōveris   d. cēperint

_____6. a. nōn vis   b. feram   c. lacrimāmus   d. mūnit

_____7. a. ēgerātis   b. fēcerant   c. poteram   d. īverat

_____8. a. it   b. audīvit   c. vident   d. curritis

_____9. a. fuī   b. facit   c. mōvistis   d. sēnsimus

__ 10.   a. rīdēbō   b. volam   c. sedent   d. erunt

PRACTICE THREE

Select the correct English translation for the following verb forms. Place the letter of your answer in the blanks provided.

_____1. terret   a. she had scared   b. she is scaring   c. she will scare

_____2. pugnāveram   a. I have fought   b. I was fighting   c. I had fought

_____3. dūcētis   a. You will lead   b. You will have led   c. You do lead

_____4. poteram   a. I had been able   b. I was able   c. I will be able

_____5. fueris   a. You will be   b. You will have been   c. You have been

_____6. finīte   a. Finished   b. You will finish   c. Finish!

_____7. habēbāmus   a. We used to have   b. We have had   c. We will have

_____8. ambulāre   a. Walk!   b. to walk   c. Don't walk

_____9. Nōlī cantāre a. Do Sing   b. You are singing   c. Don't sing!

__ 10. cēpimus   a. We did take   b. We do take   c. We were taking

PRACTICE FOUR

Complete the verb charts for the following verbs, keeping the same person and number.

sentiō, sentīre, sēnsī
pōnō, pōnere, posuī
eō, īre, īvī

habitō, habitāre, habitāvī
mordeō, mordēre, momordī
ferō, ferre, tulī

Pres.	_____	pōnitis _____	_____
Imperf.	_____	_____	_____
Fut.	_____	_____	_____
Perf.	sēnsimus	_____	_____
Pluperf.	_____	_____	īverās _____
Fut. Perf.	_____	_____	_____
Pres.	_____	_____	_____
Imperf.	habitābant	_____	_____
Fut.	_____	mordēbit _____	_____
Perf.	_____	_____	_____
Pluperf.	_____	_____	_____
Fut. Perf.	_____	_____	tulerō _____

PRACTICE FIVE

*Select the best answer from **a**, **b**, **c**, or **d**. Place the letter of your answer in the blank provided.*

_____1. Diū Antōnius in forum <u>remained</u>.

    a. mānsī   b. manēbat   c. manē   d. mānserat

_____2. Antōnī, <u>hurry</u> domum!

    a. festīnā   b. festīnāte   c. festīnāre   d. festīnās

_____3. Mea māter <u>erat</u> fīlia senātōris.

    a. is   b. had been   c. will be   d. was

_____4. Crās, nostrum iter <u>we will have finished.</u>

    a. complēbimus   b. complēverimus   c. complēverāmus   d. complēmus

_____5. Nunc ancillae in trīclīnium cibum <u>will bring</u>.

    a. tulērunt   b. ferunt   c. feram   d. ferent

_____6. Patrī Rōmam statim <u>redīre</u> necesse est.

    a. will return   b. returns   c. to return   d. had returned

_____7. Puella, cur tam celeriter <u>curris</u>?

    a. is she running   b. are you running   c. will you run   d. did she run

_____8. Ego novam stolam tibi emere <u>wish</u>.

    a. voluī   b. voluistis   c. volō   d. velle

_____9. Who <u>will lead</u> you to school in the morning?

    a. dūcēbat   b. dūcēs   c. dūcet   d. dūcit

___10. Hodiē in forō ōrātor longam ōrātiōnem <u>had made</u>.

    a. fēcerat   b. fēcerit   c. facit   d. fēcerant

___11. Poterat : posse :: _____ agere

    a. ēgerat   b. agēbat   c. aget   d. ēgit

___12. Pater multās epistulās <u>to write</u> parat.

    a. scrīpsit   b. nōlī scrībere   c. scrībere   d. scrībēbat

___13. Rufe, <u>custōdī</u> vestīmenta!

    a. guard   b. guards   c. was guarding   d. don't guard

___14. Manē servī in agrīs <u>used to work.</u>

    a. labōrābant   b. labōrāvērunt   c. labōrant   d. labōrābātis

___ 15. _____ : rēxerō :: tenēbō : tenuerō

    a. Regō   b. Regēbam   c. Regam   d. Regere

___ 16. Canēs, tuum dominum <u>don't bite</u>!

    a. nōlīte mordēre   b. nōlī mordēre   c. mordēbitis   d. mordēte

___ 17. The cook <u>did prepare</u> an excellent meal.

    a. parāvit   b. parāvistī   c. parat   d. parābat

___ 18. Ubi <u>will I find</u> tabernam laniī?

    a. inveniō   b. inveniam   c. inveniēs   d. inveniēbam

___ 19. You <u>can make </u>the journey in just a few hours.

    a. facere potes   b. facis posse   c. facis   d. potes

___ 20. Caesar celeriter ad prōvinciam <u>ībat</u>.

    a. had gone   b. did go   c. used to go   d. will go

PART 5

Verbs - Passive Voice

CHAPTER I — THE PRESENT PASSIVE SYSTEM

WHAT IS PASSIVE VOICE?

The passive voice is used when the subjective of a sentence is receiving the action instead of performing the action.

Active Voice - the subject performs the action.

Canis virum mordet.   *The dog bites the man.*

Passive Voice - the subject receives the action.

Vir ā cane mordētur.   *The man is bitten by the dog.*

Remember that the person or animal that is performing the action in a passive voice construction takes the Ablative Case and is known as an **Ablative of Agent**.

FORMATION AND TRANSLATION OF THE PRESENT PASSIVE SYSTEM

The passive forms of the present, imperfect, and future tenses are formed in the same manner as their active counterparts except for the personal verb endings. In the present system (present, imperfect and future tenses), passive voice is indicated by special personal verb endings. Look at the chart below.

Personal Verb Endings for Present System Passive					
Singular			*Plural*		
English Pronoun	Latin Verb Ending	Latin Pronoun	English Pronoun	Latin Verb Ending	Latin Pronoun
I	**-(o)r**	Ego	*We*	**-mur**	Nōs
You	**-ris**	Tū	*You*	**-minī**	Vōs
He, She, It	**-tur**	Is, Ea, Id	*They*	**-ntur**	Eī, Eae, Ea

PRESENT TENSE PASSIVE

Present Stem + Regular Passive Personal verb endings:

I	II	III	IIIio	IV
amō, amāre, amāvī, amātus	doceō, docēre, docuī, doctus	regō, regere, rēxī, rectus	capiō, capere, cēpī, captus	mūniō, mūnīre, mūnīvī, mūnītus
amor	doceor	regor	capior	mūnior
amāris	docēris	regeris	caperis	mūnīris
amātur	docētur	regitur	capitur	mūnītur
amāmur	docēmur	regimur	capimur	mūnīmur
amāminī	docēminī	regiminī	capiminī	mūnīminī
amantur	docentur	reguntur	capiuntur	mūniuntur

Translation: I am _____ed, I am being _____ed

NOTA BENE:
For 3rd conjugation verbs, the linking vowel -i changes to -e before the 2nd person singular personal verb ending -ris.

IMPERFECT TENSE PASSIVE

Present Stem + bā + Regular Passive Personal verb endings:

I	II	III	IIIio	IV
amō, amāre, amāvī, amātus	doceō, docēre, docuī, doctus	regō, regere, rēxī, rectus	capiō, capere, cēpī, captus	mūniō, mūnīre, mūnīvī, mūnītus
amābar	docēbar	regēbar	capiēbar	mūniēbar
amābāris	docēbāris	regēbāris	capiēbāris	mūniēbāris
amābātur	docēbatur	regēbātur	capiēbātur	mūniēbātur
amābāmur	docēbāmur	regēbāmur	capiēbāmur	mūniēbāmur
amābāminī	docēbāminī	regēbāminī	capiēbāminī	mūniēbāminī
amābantur	docēbantur	regēbantur	capiēbantur	mūniēbantur

Translation: I was _____ed, I was being _____ed, I kept on being _____ed
I used to be _____ed, I began to be _____ed

FUTURE TENSE PASSIVE

Present Stem + bō, bi, bu's + Passive Personal endings for 1st & 2nd conjugations

Present Stem + 1 a and 5 e's + Passive Personal endings for 3rd conjugation

Present Stem + 1 ia and 5 ie's + Passive Personal endings for 3rd io & 4th conjugations

I amō, amāre, amāvī, amātus	II doceō, docēre, docuī, doctus	III regō, regere, rēxī, rectus	IIIio capiō, capere, cēpī, captus	IV mūniō, mūnīre, mūnīvī, mūnītus
amābor	docēbor	regar	capiar	mūniar
amāberis	docēberis	regēris	capiēris	mūniēris
amābitur	docēbitur	regētur	capiētur	mūniētur
amābimur	docēbimur	regēmur	capiēmur	mūniēmur
amābiminī	docēbiminī	regēminī	capiēminī	mūniēminī
amābuntur	docēbuntur	regentur	capientur	mūnientur

Translation: I will be_____ed

NOTA BENE:
For 1st and 2nd conjugation verbs, the tense sign -bi- changes to -be-before the 2nd person singular personal verb ending -ris.
The way to distinguish between the 2nd person singular of the present and future of 3rd conjugation verbs is to note the quantity of the linking vowel:
regeris *you are ruled* (Present) regēris *you will be ruled* (Future)

THE PRESENT PASSIVE INFINITIVE

The present passive infinitive is formed from the second principal part of the verb. For 1st, 2nd, and 4th conjugation verbs you change the final -e to an -ī. For 3rd conjugation verbs, you drop the -ere and replace it with an -ī.

Active Infinitive	English Meaning	Passive Infinitive	English Meaning
amāre	*to love*	amārī	*to be loved*
docēre	*to teach*	docērī	*to be taught*
regere	*to rule*	regī	*to be ruled*
capere	*to seize*	capī	*to be seized*
mūnīre	*to fortify*	mūnīrī	*to be fortified*

PRACTICE ONE

Change each of the following verb forms to the passive voice keeping the same person and number. Translate both the active and passive verb forms into English. The first one has been done for you.

1. <u>portābunt</u>   <u>portābuntur</u>

    <u>They will carry</u>   <u>They will be carried</u>

2. <u>cupiēbāmus</u>   _____

    _____   _____

3. <u>fert</u>   _____

    _____   _____

4. <u>admittet</u>   _____

    _____   _____

5. <u>dōnō</u>   _____

    _____   _____

6. <u>trahēs</u>   _____

    _____   _____

7. <u>pōnis</u>   _____

    _____   _____

8   <u>agunt</u>   _____

    _____   _____

9. <u>dīcere</u>   _____

    _____   _____

(cont.)

10. vidēbit _____ _____

_____ _____

11. commovēbātis _____ _____

_____ _____

12. dīcam _____ _____

_____ _____

13. punīre _____ _____

_____ _____

PRACTICE TWO
Keeping the same person and number, complete the verb charts for the following verbs

moneō, monēre, monuī, monitus   iurō, iurāre, iurāvī, iurātus
gerō, gerere, gessī, gestum   pūniō, pūnīre, pūnīvī, pūnītus
ferō, ferre, tulī, lātus   excipiō, excipere, excēpī, exceptus

Pres.	_____	geritur _____	_____
Imperf.	monēbāmur _____	_____	_____
Fut.	_____	_____	ferar _____

Pres.	iurāminī _____	_____	_____
Imperf.	_____	_____	excipiēbantur _____
Fut.	_____	pūniēris _____	_____

PRACTICE THREE

Change the verb in the active voice to the passive, making all necessary changes in the sentence. Then translate the second sentence into English.

1. In thermīs servus vestīmenta custodiēbat. In thermīs vestīmenta ā servō

    custōdiēba_____ . _____

    _____

2. Mors gladiātōris tē commovet. Tū morte gladiātōris commove_____ . _____

    _____

3. Ancilla togās dominī in cistā pōnet. Togae dominī in cistā ab ancillā

    pōnē_____ . _____

    _____

4. Meus pater mē ad Circum dūcet. Ego ad Circum ā patre dūc_____ . _____

    _____

PRACTICE FOUR

Underline all subjects and circle all ablatives of agent. Then translate the following sentences into English.

1. Paedagōgus puerōs ad lūdum dūcit. Puerī ā paedagōgō ad lūdum dūcuntur.___

    _____

    _____

2. Nova stola ab ancillā faciēbātur. Ancilla novam stolam faciēbat. _____

    _____

    _____

3. Pecūnia cīvis ā praedōnibus capiētur. Praedōnēs pecūniam cīvis capient._____

    _____

    _____

4. Pāstor animālia cūrat. Animālia ā pāstōre cūrantur. _____

    _____

    _____

(cont.)

5. Līberī sordidās manūs lavābant. Dīligenter sordidae manūs ā līberīs lavābantur. _____

_____

6. Nostrī mīlitēs hostēs vincent. Hostēs ā nostrīs mīlitibus vincentur. _____

_____

_____

7. Īrāta domina timidam ancillam commovēbit. Timida ancilla ab īrātā dominā commovēbitur. _____

_____

8. Magnum incendium mē terret. Magnō incendiō terreor. _____

_____

_____

CHAPTER II — THE PERFECT PASSIVE SYSTEM

· ·

FORMATION AND TRANSLATION OF THE PERFECT PASSIVE SYSTEM

The Perfect System Passive (perfect, pluperfect, and future perfect) uses the fourth principal part of the verb plus a form of the Latin verb **esse**. From the 4th principal part of the verb we learn the gender and number of the subject of the sentence. From the form of the verb **esse**, we learn the tense and also the number of the verb.

Mulier ā canibus morsa est.	*The woman was bitten by the dogs.*
Mīlitēs ā canibus morsī sunt.	*The soldiers were bitten by the dogs.*

The following chart is useful for learning the correct endings for the fourth principal part.

Gender of Subject	Singular Subject	Plural Subject
Mas.	-us	-ī
Fem.	-a	-ae
Neut.	-um	-a

THE PERFECT TENSE PASSIVE

4th principal part + present tense forms of **sum, esse**:

I	II	III
amō, amāre, amāvī, <u>amā</u>tus	doceō, docēre, docuī, <u>doctus</u>	regō, regere, rēxī, <u>rēctus</u>
amātus, -a sum	doctus, -a sum	rēctus, -a sum
amātus, -a es	doctus, -a es	rēctus, -a es
amātus, -a, um est	doctus, -a, -um est	rēctus, -a, est
amātī, -ae sumus	doctī, -ae sumus	rēctī, -ae sumus
amātī, -ae estis	doctī, -ae estis	rēctī, -ae, estis
amātī, -ae, -a sunt	doctī, -ae, -a sunt	rēctī, -ae, a sunt

III io	IV
capiō, capere,	mūniō, mūnīre,
cēpī, <u>capt</u>us	mūnīvī, <u>mūnī</u>tus
captus, -a sum	mūnītus, -a sum
captus, -a es	mūnītus, -a es
captus, -a, -um est	mūnītus, -a, -um est
captī, -ae sumus	mūnītī, -ae sumus
captī, -ae estis	mūnītī, -ae estis
captī, -ae, -a sunt	mūnītī, -ae, -a sunt

Translation: I was_____ed, I have been_____ed

THE PLUPERFECT TENSE PASSIVE

4th principal part + imperfect tense forms of **sum, esse**:

I	II	III
amō, amāre,	doceō, docēre,	regō, regere,
amāvī, <u>amā</u>tus	docuī, <u>doct</u>us	rēxī, <u>rēc</u>tus
amātus, -a eram	doctus, -a eram	rēctus, -a eram
amātus, -a erās	doctus, -a erās	rēctus, -a erās
amātus, -a, um erat	doctus, -a -um erat	rēctus, -a, -um erat
amātī, -ae erāmus	doctī, -ae erāmus	rēctī, -ae erāmus
amātī, -ae erātis	doctī, -ae erātis	rēctī, -ae erātis
amātī, -ae, -a erant	doctī, -ae, -a erant	rēctī, -ae, a erant

III io	IV
capiō, capere,	mūniō, mūnīre,
cēpī, <u>capt</u>us	mūnīvī, <u>mūnī</u>tus
captus, -a eram	mūnītus, -a eram
captus, -a erās	mūnītus, -a erās
captus, -a, -um erat	mūnītus, -a, -um erat
captī, -ae erāmus	mūnītī, -ae erāmus
captī, -ae erātis	mūnītī, -ae erātis
captī, -ae, -a erant	mūnītī, -ae, -a erant

Translation: I had been_____ed

THE FUTURE PERFECT TENSE PASSIVE

4th principal part + future tense forms of **sum, esse:**

I	**II**	**III**
amō, amāre,	doceō, docēre,	regō, regere,
amāvī, <u>amāt</u>us	docuī, <u>doct</u>us	rēxī, <u>rēct</u>us

amātus, -a erō	doctus, -a, erō	rēctus, -a erō
amātus, -a eris	doctus, -a eris	rēctus, -a eris
amātus, -a um erit	doctus, -a -um erit	rēctus, -a, -um erit
amātī, -ae erimus	doctī, -ae erimus	rēctī, -ae erimus
amātī, -ae eritis	doctī, -ae eritis	rēctī, -ae eritis
amātī, -ae, -a erunt	doctī, -ae, -a erunt	rēctī, -ae, -a erunt

III io	**IV**
capiō, capere,	mūniō, mūnīre,
cēpī, <u>capt</u>us	mūnīvī, <u>mūnīt</u>us

captus, -a erō	mūnītus, -a erō
captus, -a eris	mūnītus, -a eris
captus, -a, um erit	mūnītus, -a, -um erit
captī, -ae erimus	mūnītī, -ae erimus
captī, -ae eritis	mūnītī, -ae eritis
captī, -ae, -a erunt	mūnītī, -ae, -a erunt

Translation: I will have been_____ed

NOTA BENE:
   Remember that the neuter forms of the verbs can only occur in the 3rd person singular and plural.

PRACTICE ONE

Change each of the following verb forms to the passive voice keeping the same tense, person, number, and gender. The stem of the fourth principal part has been provided for you. Translate both the active and passive verb forms into English. The first one has been done for you.

1. laudāverit (m.)   laudātus erit

   He will have praised   He will have been praised

2. fēcērunt (n.)   fact

3. conspēxerint (f.)   conspect

4. dōnāverāmus (f.)   dōnāt

5. ēgerātis (m)   act

6. terruistī (f.)   territ

7. audīvī (m.)   audīt

8. traxit (n.)   tract

9. invēnerāmus (m.)   invent

10. <u>posuerō (f.)</u> _____   <u>posit</u> _____

_____   _____

11. <u>docuerātis (m.)</u> _____   <u>doct</u> _____

_____   _____

12. <u>tuleris (f.)</u> _____   <u>lāt</u> _____

_____   _____

13. <u>pūnīvit (f.)</u> _____   <u>pūnīt</u> _____

_____   _____

14. <u>cēpimus (m.)</u> _____   <u>capt</u> _____

_____   _____

15. <u>vīderam (f.)</u> _____   <u>vīs</u> _____

_____   _____

PRACTICE TWO

Keeping the same person, number, and gender, complete the verb charts for the following verbs.

pugnō, pugnāre, pugnāvī, pugnātus   **teneō, tenēre, tenuī, tentus**
mittō, mittere, mīsī, missus   **videō, vidēre, vīdī, vīsus**
custōdiō, custōdīre, custōdīvī, custōdītus **dēfendō, dēfendere, dēfendī, dēfēnsus**

Perf.	_____	_____	<u>custōdīta sunt</u>
Pluperf.	_____	missae erāmus	_____
Fut. Perf.	<u>pugnātum erit</u>	_____	_____

Perf.	_____	vīsī estis	_____
Pluperf.	<u>tenta eram</u>	_____	_____
Fut. Perf.	_____	_____	<u>dēfēnsus eris</u>

PRACTICE THREE

Underline all subjects and circle all ablatives of agent. Then translate the following sentences into English.

1. Magister discipulōs laudāverat. Discipulī ā magistrō laudātī erant._____

   _____

   _____

2. Senātōrēs ā prīncipe Rōmam vocātī sunt. Prīnceps senātōrēs Rōmam vocāvit.___

   _____

   _____

3. Multa carmina ā poētīs in forō recitāta erunt. Poētae multa carmina in forō

   recitāverint._____

   _____

   _____

4. Haec fābula tē commōvit. Tū hāc fābulā commōtus es._ _____

   _____

   _____

5. Meus dominus scelestōs servōs nōn verberāverat. Scelestī servī ā meō dominō

   nōn verberātī erant._____

   _____

   _____

PRACTICE FOUR

Select the correct subject to agree with the verb in each sentence. Place the letter of your answer in the blank.

____1. _____ in viā vīsus erat.

      a. Patrēs   b. Māter   c. Mīles   d. Plaustrum

____2. _____ in tabernā laniī emptus est.

      a. Porcus   b. Porcī   c. Mappa   d. Ōva

____3. _____ in aliā tabernā empta sunt.

      a. Carō   b. Pictūrae   c. Mēnsa   d. Holera

_____4. _____ a mātre vocātae sunt.

     a. Frāter   b. Puerī   c. Sorōrēs   d. Fīlia

_____5. _____ a mātre vocātī sunt.

     a. Mīlitēs   b. Antōnius   c. Claudia   d. Vir

_____6. _____ ad domum parēntum missa erat.

     a. Uxōrēs   b. Marītus   c. Uxor   d. Frātrēs

_____7. _____ in hāc villā inventa erat.

     a. Gladius   b. Epistula   c. Statuae   d. Ōrnāmenta

_____8. _____ in silvā vīsī erant.

     a. Canis et lupus   b. Equus   c. Mīles   d. Sīgnum

PRACTICE FIVE

Select the correct verb form to agree with the subject in each sentence. Place the letter of your answer in the lefthand blank.

_____1. In illā tabernā multī librī _____.

     a. vēnditus est   b. vēndita est   c. vēndita sunt   d. venditī sunt.

_____2. Multī praeclārī senātōrēs ad nostram cēnam_____.

     a. invitātī erant   b. invitātus est   c. invitātae sunt   d. invitātum erit

_____3. In bellō multa vulnera ab imperātōre_____.

     a. acceptī erant   b. accepta erat   c. accepta erant   d. acceptus erat

_____4. Victōria in Curiā ā prīncipe_____.

     a. nūntiāta sunt   b. nūntiāta est   c. nūntiātī sunt   d. nūntiātum est

_____5. Cur vōs ad portam nōn_____?

     a. exceptī estis   b. exceptus es   c. exceptae sunt   d. excepta sum

_____6. Vetus gladiātor in arēnā_____.

     a. victus erat   b. victa eram   c. victī erant   d. victa erat

_____7. Diū pīrātae ā nostrīs nautīs_____.

     a. conspectae sunt   b. conspectī sum   c. conspectī sunt   d. conspecta es

_____8. Grave onus ā fortissimō servō_____.

     a. mōtus erit   b. mōtum erit   c. mōta erit   d. mōta erunt

CHAPTER III — REVIEW OF ALL TENSES
OF THE INDICATIVE PASSIVE

. . . .

PRACTICE ONE

Underline the stems of the following verb forms. Match these verb forms and meanings.
Use stems to help identify tenses! You will not use all your answers.

pellō, pellere, pepulī, pulsus, *to push*

_____1. pulsum erit   a. to be pushed

_____2. pulsa erat   b. He is pushed

_____3. pellī   c. He will be pushed

_____4. pellitur   d. She had been pushed

_____5. pellētur   e. They had been pushed

_____6. pellēbātur   f. It will have been pushed

                             g. It was being pushed

terreō, terrēre, terruī, territus, *to frighten*

_____1. terrēbimur   a. We are frightened

_____2. terrēmur   b. We will have been frightened

_____3. territī sumus   c. We used to be frightened

_____4. terrēbāmur   d. to be frightened

_____5. territī erāmus   e. We have been frightened

_____6. terrērī   f. We will be frightened

                             g. We had been frightened

PRACTICE TWO

Give the person, number, tense, and translation of each of the following verb forms. The first one is done for you.

		Per.	Num.	Tense	Translation
1.	salūtātī estis	2	pl.	perf.	you were greeted
2.	mittar				
3.	fertur				
4.	vidēberis				
5.	pūnita eram				
6.	parāta erit				
7.	monēris				
8.	vocābiminī				
9.	capta sunt				
10.	regēminī				
11.	audītus erās				
12.	portāta sunt				
13.	regimur				
14.	laudābantur				
15.	mūnītum erat				

PRACTICE THREE

Complete the verb charts for the following verbs keeping the same person, number, voice, and gender.

audiō, audīre, audīvī, audītus
spectō, spectāre, spectāvī, spectātus
fundō, fundere, fūdī, fūsus

ferō, ferre, tulī, lātus
legō, legere, lēgī, lēctus
permoveō, permovēre, permōvī, permōtus

Pres.	_____	_____	_____
Imperf.	_____	_____	_____
Fut.	_____	spectāberis	_____
Perf.	_____	_____	fūsum est
Pluperf.	audītae erāmus	_____	_____
Fut. Perf.	_____	_____	_____

(cont.)

Pres.	_____	_____	permoveor _____
Imperf.	_____	legēbantur _____	_____
Fut.	_____	_____	_____
Perf.	_____	_____	_____
Pluperf.	_____	_____	_____
Fut. Perf.	lātī eritis _____	_____	_____

PRACTICE FOUR

Select the best answer from a, b, c, or d. Place the letter of your answer in the space provided.

_____1. Pecus magnum ab hōc pāstōre multōs annōs <u>had been cared for</u>.

    a. cūrātus erat   b. cūrātum est   c. cūrātum erat   d. cūrābātur

_____2. The slave did not wish <u>to be sent</u> to the mines.

    a. mittere   b. missus est   c. mitte   d. mittī

_____3. Fūrēs <u>will be punished</u>.

    a. pūniētur   b. pūnītī erunt   c. pūnientur   d. pūnient

_____4. Ego ā ferōcī cane <u>was bitten</u>.

    a. morsus eram   b. morsum est   c. morsa sum   d. mordēbor

_____5. Rēx verbīs ōrāculī <u>terrētur</u>.

    a. has been frightened   c. will frighten
    b. is frightened   d. will be frightened

_____6. The money <u>can be given</u> to the pirates right away.

    a. potest dārī   b. poterat dārī   c. dātur   d. possunt

_____7. Bellum ab hostibus contrā sociōs nostrōs <u>gestum est</u>.

    a. is waged   b. will be waged   c. has been waged   d. waged

_____8. Māgnificī lūdī ā prīncipe datī erant.

    a. Magnificent games were being given by the emperor.
    b. Magnificent games had been given by the emperor.
    c. Magnificent games for the emperor had been given.
    d. They had given magnificent games for the emperor.

_____9. Gemmae et vestēs pulchrae puellīs <u>ostendēbantur</u>.

    a. will be displayed   c. had been displayed
    b. were being displayed   d. are being displayed

____10. capitur : captum erit :: fertur :_____

    a. lātum erat   b. lātum erit   c. lātum est   d. ferētur

CHAPTER IV — REVIEW OF ALL TENSES
OF
THE INDICATIVE ACTIVE AND PASSIVE
. . . .

PRACTICE ONE
Fill in the blanks of this exercise in order to review some basic fact about verbs.

1. How many verb conjugations are there in Latin? _____

2. Give the infinitive endings of the conjugations.

   _____   _____   _____   _____

3. Name the six tenes of the verb in Latin.   _____   _____

   _____   _____   _____   _____

4. The <u>voices</u> of a Latin verb are the_____ and the_____.

5. To find the present stem of a Latin verb, drop the _____ from the

   present_____.

6. How is the present stem related to the present imperative?_____

   _____

7. What is the rule for the imperative plural of the 1st, 2nd and 4th conjugations?

   of the 3rd?_____

8. Give the passive infinitive endings of the four conjugations.

   _____   _____   _____   _____

9. What is the tense sign of the imperfect tense?_____

10. What two irregular verbs have a different tense sign for the imperfect tense.

    _____   _____

11. What is the tense sign of the future tense in the 1st & 2nd conjugations?_____

    In the 3rd?_____ in the 3rd io and 4th?_____

12. To find the perfect active stem of a Latin verb, drop_____ from the_____

    principal part of the verb.

13. List the perfect active endings. _____

14. What three letters are the tense sign of the pluperfect tense? _____

15. What three letters are the tense sign of the future perfect tense? _____

SYNOPSIS OF THE VERB

A quick way to look at a whole verb is the **synopsis** (a "look together" of all the tenses), in which all the forms active and passive are given for one person and number.

audiō - *I hear*	audīre - *to hear*	<u>4</u>
audīvī - *I heard*	audītus - *having been heard*	

	active	meaning		passive	meaning
Pres.	**audit**	he hears		**audītur**	he is being heard
Imperf.	**audiēbat**	he was hearing		**audiēbatur**	he was being heard
Future	**audiet**	he will hear		**audiētur**	he will be heard
Perf.	**audīvit**	he heard		**audītus est**	he was heard
Pluperf.	**audīverat**	he had heard		**audītus erat**	he had been heard
Fut. Perf.	**audīverit**	he will have heard		**audītus erit**	he will have been heard

sum - *I am*	esse - *to be*	<u>irr</u>
fuī - *I was*		

	active	meaning
Pres.	**sunt**	they are
Imperf.	**erant**	they used to be
Future	**erunt**	they will be
Perf.	**fuērunt**	they were
Pluperf.	**fuerant**	they had been
Fut. Perf.	**fuerint**	they will have been

PRACTICE TWO

Fill in each chart with its assigned verb. Use the verb charts on page one hundred sixty-eight as your model.

1. PRINCIPAL PARTS: dēleō, dēlēre, dēlēvī, dēlētus, *to destroy* (3rd sing.)

	active	meaning		passive	meaning
Pres.					
Imperf.					
Future					
Perf.					
Pluperf.					
Fut. Perf.					

2. PRINCIPAL PARTS: laudō, laudāre, laudāvī, laudātus, *to praise* (2nd sing.)

	active	meaning		passive	meaning
Pres.					
Imperf.					
Future					
Perf.					
Pluperf.					
Fut. Perf.					

(cont.)

3. PRINCIPAL PARTS: pūniō, pūnīre, pūnīvī, pūnītus, *to punish* (1st pl.)

	active	meaning		passive	meaning
Pres.					
Imperf.					
Future					
Perf.					
Pluperf.					
Fut. Perf.					

4. PRINCIPAL PARTS: dīco, dīcere, dīxī, dictus, *to tell* (3rd pl.)

	active	meaning		passive	meaning
Pres.					
Imperf.					
Future					
Perf.					
Pluperf.					
Fut. Perf.					

5. PRINCIPAL PARTS: volō, velle, voluī, *to wish* (2nd pl.)

	active	meaning
Pres.		
Imperf.		
Future		
Perf.		
Pluperf.		
Fut. Perf.		

6. PRINCIPAL PARTS: possum, posse, potuī, *to be able* (1st sing.)

	active	meaning
Pres.		
Imperf.		
Future		
Perf.		
Pluperf.		
Fut. Perf.		

PRACTICE THREE

Give the person, number, tense, voice, and translation of each of the vollowing verb forms. The first one is done for you.

	Per.	Num.	Tense	Voice	Translation
1. frangitur	3	sing.	pres.	pass.	it is broken
2. monēbam					
3. vocāberis					
4. poteris					
5. fuerāmus					
6. reprehendō					
7. regent					
8. petītae sumus					
9. poterint					
10. facitis					
11. nōluērunt					
12. feritur					
13. terrēmus					
14. acta erant					
15. cupīvīmus					
16. dōnāveris					
17. erātis					
18. vidēbar					
19. lāta est					
20. sentiam					
21. ībant					
22. audīminī					
23. dūceris					
24. volam					
25. spectās					

PRACTICE FOUR

*Identify the one verb that is **not** in the same **tense** or **mood** as the other verbs. Place the letter of your answer in the space provided.*

____1. a. regēmur b. vidēs c. vocant d. caperis

____2. a. īverō b. posuērunt c. sēderis d. lātum erit

____3. a. cupī b. ferre c. tenēre d. audī

____4. a. nōlam b. timēs c. cantābunt d. petēminī

____5. a. velle b. mittī c. parāre d. nōlī īre

____6. a. cēpimus b. facit c. mutāta sunt d. demōnstrāvī

____7. a. agī b. dīc c. clamāte d. invenī

____8. a. lacrimāverātis b. facta erant c. poteram d. pūnīta eram

____9. a. nōlīte cēlāre b. fers c. sentīte d. ī

___10. a. ībō b. finiēbantur c. dūcēbam d. erāmus

PRACTICE FIVE

These verb forms are missing their stems. Choose the correct stem to complete the forms that match the translation.

scrībō, scrībere, scrīpsī, scrīptus

1. Multae epistulae ā patre_____ae erant.
   Many letters had been written by father.

2. Pater multās epistulās_____it.
   Father is writing many letters.

3. Multae epistulae ā patre_____ī debent.
   Many letters ought to be written by father.

4. Pater multās epistulās_____it.
   Father did write many letters.

5. Multae epistulae ā patre_____entur.
   Many letters will be written by father.

6. Pater multās epistulās_____erint.
   Father will have written many letters.

7. Pater multās epistulās_____re vult.
   Father wishes to write many letters.

(cont.)

8. Multae epistulae ā patre_____ae sunt.
   Many letters have been written by father.

9. Pater multās epistulās_____ēbat.
   Father used to write many letters.

10. Hodiē, pater, nōlī_____ re multās epistulās.
    Today, father, don't write many letters.

PRACTICE SIX

Select the best answer from a, b, c, or d. Place the letter of your answer in the space provided.

____1. Haec bellica urbs <u>will be destroyed</u>.

    a. dēlētur   b. dēlēbor   c. dēlēbāmur   d. dēlēbitur

____2. Cupere : cupī :: invenīre :_____.

    a. invenī   b. invenīte   c. invēneris   d. invenīrī

____3. _____ ab illīs mīlitibus custōdītī sunt.

    a. Uxōrēs   b. Senātōrēs   c. Gladiātor   d. Pīrāta

____4. He <u>used to live</u> in Rome.

    a. habitat   b. habitāvit   c. habitāre   d. habitābat

____5. Animus fugitīvī <u>will be shattered</u>.

    a. frangētur   b. fractus erit   c. frangēbātur   d. frangitur

____6. Cook, <u>prepare</u> the dinner now!

    a. parat   b. parā   c. nōlī parāre   d. parāte

____7. Cēlās : cēlā ::_____ : fer

    a. ferte   b. ferēs   c. tulī   d. fers

____8. Tū, captīvus noster, Rōmam <u>nōn dūcēris</u>.

    a. will not be led   b. are not being led   c. were not led   d. will not lead

____9. He tries <u>to swim</u> everyday.

    a. natābat   b. natāre   c. natāre potest   d. natā

___10. Mox tōta finis nostrae prōvinciae ab explōrātōribus_____.

    a. vīsus erit   b. vīsī erunt   c. vidēbāris   d. vīsa erit

___11. The tunics <u>had been placed</u> in the trunks.

    a. positae sunt   b. posita erat   c. positae erant   d. pōnēbant

___ 12. Why does that boy not wish <u>to be seen</u> by his father?

    a. vidērī   b. vidē   c. vidēre   d. vidētur

___ 13. Puellae patrī fābulam narrāvērunt.

    a. The girls were told a story by their father.
    b. The fathers had told a story to the girls.
    c. The girls told a story to their father.
    d. They were telling the father's story to the girl.

___ 14. <u>I can give</u> you the money.

    a. potuī   b. dōnāre possum   c. dōnō   d. dōnāre poterō

___ 15. _____ incendiō vastāta sunt.

    a. Villa   b. Onus   c. Aedificia   d. Pictūrae

___ 16. Claudia, <u>you will spin</u> wool today!

    a. trahe   b. trahis   c. traxistī   d. trahēs

___ 17. Nāvēs ā pīrātīs saepe <u>petītae erant</u>.

    a. had been attacked   c. had been attacking
    b. had attacked   d. were being attacked

___ 18. _____, hīc statim venī!

    a. Serve   b. Servī   c. Servus   d. Servō

___ 19. Nōs lectīcā in urbem ferēmur.

    a. We will carry the litter into the city.
    b. We are being carried by litter into the city.
    c. We will be carried by litter into the city.
    d. The litter will carry them into the ciy.

___ 20. Infāns placidē <u>dormit</u>.

    a. will sleep   b. has slept   c. is sleeping   d. began to sleep

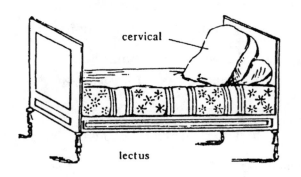

cervical

lectus

Review of All Grammar

PRACTICE ONE

Select the best answer from a, b, c, or d. Place the letter of your answer in the space provided.

_____ 1. <u>Slave</u>, celeriter labōrā!

     a. Servī   b. Servōs   c. Serve   d. Servus

_____ 2. Epistulās _____ scrīpsī.

     a. stilum   b. stilō   c. stilī   d. stilōrum

_____ 3. Hodiē Antōnius et Lucius sunt _____.

     a. dēfessōs   b. dēfessus   c. dēfessī   d. dēfessum

_____ 4. Octō minus quinque sunt _____.

     a. duo   b. sex   c. trēs   d. decem

_____ 5. Erāmus : fuimus :: _____ : mānsērunt

     a. manent   b. manēbant   c. manēbat   d. manēbunt

_____ 6. _____ sunt magna.

     a. Templa   b. Templō   c. Templum   d. Templī

_____ 7. Meus patruus multōs lūdōs <u>spectāvit</u>.

     a. has watched   b. used to watch   c. will watch   d. is watching

_____ 8. Puer <u>sub arbore</u> sedet.

     a. in the trees   b. above the tree   c. near the tree   d. under the tree

_____ 9. For a very long time we <u>were</u> very worried about you.

     a. fuimus   b. erimus   c. erāmus   d. sumus

_____ 10. The slave <u>slowly</u> walked towards the forum.

     a. lentus   b. lentē   c. lentum   d. lentī

_____ 11. Semper tē <u>in memoriā tenēbō</u>.

     a. I did remember   b. I do remember   c. I will remember   d. I remembered

_____ 12. Servī, celeriter cistās <u>in raedā</u> pōnite!

     a. in the carriage   c. into the carriage

     b. out of the carriage   d. under the carriage

___ 13. Antōnius in hortō _____ videt.

   a. amicī   b. puellārum   c. puella   d. puellam

___ 14. Quō iter faciēbant? Nōs _____ iter faciēbāmus.

   a. ē villā   b. ab oppidō   c. in urbe   d. ad oppidum

___ 15. Children, <u>don't shout</u>! You will wake up your father.

   a. nōn clamant b. nōlīte clamāre c. clamāte d. nōlī clamāre

___ 16. Pecūniam <u>virō</u> nōn dedimus.

   a. of the man b. with the man c. to the man d. about the man

___ 17. Coquusne cibum parat?

   a. Is the cook preparing the food? c. Did the cook prepare the food?
   b. The cook is preparing the food. d. Will the cook prepare the food.

___ 18. Agrī <u>agricolārum</u> erant magnī.

   a. farmers b. of the farmers c. of the farmer d. to the farmer

___ 19. She <u>used to live</u> near us.

   a. habitābat b. habitāvit c. habitat d. habitābit

___ 20. Cūr tua mater est _____ ?

   a. īrātus b. īrātam c. īrāta d. īrātā

PRACTICE TWO

Select the best answer from a, b, c, or d. Place the letter of your answer in the space provided.

_____1. Stola <u>fēminae</u> erat sordida.

    a. of the women   b. by the woman   c. woman's   d. for the women

_____2. Estis : eritis :: teneō : _____ .

    a. tenē   b. tenuī   c. tenēbam   d. tenēbō

_____3. I <u>am</u> not at all nervous about this test.

    a. eram   b. erō   c. fuī   d. sum

_____4. Boys, <u>hurry</u> home!

    a. festīnās   b. festīnāte   c. festīnant   d. festīnābātis

_____5. Ego ancillās _____ nōn amō.

    a. īgnāvās   b. īgnāvae   c. īgnāvīs   d. īgnāvam

_____6. <u>Dominum servumque</u> prope arēnam nōn vīdērunt.

    a. either the master or the slave   c. the master and the slave
    b. the master or the slave   d. both the master and the slave

_____7. The master hit the slave <u>with a stick</u>.

    a. virgā   b. virga   c. virgīs   d. virgam

_____8. Trēs plūs quattuor sunt _____ .

    a. ūnus   b. novem   c. septem   d. octō

_____9. Senātor Rōmā <u>ad prōvinciam</u> iter fēcit.

    a. to the province   c. from the province
    b. out of the province   d. through the province

_____10. Puerī <u>ex agrīs</u> cucurrērunt.

    a. in the fields   b. into the fields   c. out of the fields   d. out of the field

_____11. _____ līberōs petīvērunt.

    a. Lupum   b. Lupī   c. Lupōs   d. Lupō

_____12. Antōnia _____ parat.

    a. cantā   b. cantāre   c. cantat   d. cantāte

___ 13. Fīlī, fābulam tuō patrī nārrā!

    a. Sons, tell the story to your father!
    b. The sons tell the story to their father.
    c. Son, tell the story of your father!
    d. Son, tell the story to your father!

___ 14. Don't sit <u>on the table</u>!

    a. in mēnsā   b. dē mēnsā   c. super mēnsam   d. in mēnsam

___ 15. Pīrātae captīvōs <u>nautīs</u> crās tradent.

    a. to the sailors   b. by the sailor   c. with the sailors   d. for the sailor

___ 16. <u>Fearfully</u> the boy approached his angry father.

    a. timidus   b. timidum   c. timidē   d. timidō

___ 17. Quis multōs _____ habet?

    a. equī   b. equōs   c. equīs   d. equum

___ 18. Docēmus : docuimus :: es : _____.

    a. eras   b. fuistī   c. fuimus   d. eris

___ 19. Poēta est _____ quod prīnceps carmina nōn amat.

    a. miserae   b. miserum   c. misera   d. miser

___ 20. Crās ancillae in culīnā <u>will work</u>.

    a. labōrant   b. labōrābant   c. labōrāvērunt   d. labōrābunt

PRACTICE THREE

*Select the best answer from **a**, **b**, **c**, or **d**. Place the letter of your answer in the space provided.*

_____1. Vōs omnēs <u>have heard</u> dē victōriā nostrōrum mīlitum.

     a. audīvistis   b. audīverās   c. auditis   d. audīvistī

_____2. Pater nova aedificia _____ mōnstrābat.

     a. Antōniam   b. fīliī   c. Antōniae   d. fīliōrum

_____3. Quot pedēs habet canis?

     a. IX   b. VI   c. II   d. IV

_____4. Manē magnās _____ mercātōrum audīvimus.

     a. vōcis   b. vōcem   c. vōcum   d. vōcēs

_____5. <u>Ea</u> est mea optima amīca.

     a. She   b. He   c. Her   d. They

_____6. <u>Ubi sunt</u> molestī puerī?

     a. Where are . . . ?   b. When are . . . ?   c. Why are . . .?   d. Who are . . . ?

_____7. Mīlitēs <u>iter facere</u> volunt.

     a. make the trip   c. to make the trip
     b. makes the trip   d. had made the trip

_____8. Rēgina : rēginārum :: imperātōr : _____ .

     a. imperātōris   b. imperātōrum   c. imperātōrem   d. imperātōre

_____9. Servus magna onera ē villā <u>ad carrum</u> portābat.

     a. to the wagon   c. from the wagon
     b. into the wagon   d. around the wagon

___ 10. Omnēs gladiātōrēs <u>with great courage</u> pugnāverant.

     a. magna virtūs   c. magnā virtūte
     b. magnae virtūtēs   d. magnam virtūtem

___ 11. Hodiē omnēs _____ magnō studiō labōrant.

     a. discipulōs   b. discipula   c. discipulum   d. discipulī

___ 12. Magna : magnā :: celeris : _____ .

     a. celere   b. celerī   c. celeribus   d. celerēs

___ 13. <u>Near our house</u> est magnum flūmen.

     a. Dē nostrā villā   c. In nostrā villā
     b. Prope nostram villam   d. Per nostram villam

___ 14. <u>Gratefully</u> I accept your offer.

    a. Grātē   b. Grāta   c. Grātī   d. Grātum

___ 15. Capiēmus : cēperimus :: _____ : fueris.

    a. es   b. eras   c. eris   d. fuistī

___ 16. Miserae puellae diū <u>lacrimāverant</u>.

    a. did cry   b. were crying   c. had cried   d. are crying

___ 17. Crās nōs in forō diem_____ .

    a. agimus   b. agētis   c. agēbāmus   d. agēmus

___ 18. Via, <u>which</u> nōn est lāta, plēna plaustōrum est.

    a. quae   b. quod   c. quās   d. quī

___ 19. Turba fūrem <u>saxīs</u> verberāvit.

    a. to the rocks   b. with rocks   c. of rocks   d. without rocks

___ 20. Claudī, ferōcēs canēs _____ .

    a. cavent   b. nōlīte cavēre   c. cavē   d. cavet

PRACTICE FOUR

Select the best answer from **a, b, c,** *or* **d.** *Place the letter of your answer in the space provided.*

_____1. Nautae ad lītus <u>are swimming</u>.

    a. natābit   b. natant   c. natāverint   d. natāvērunt

_____2. Cūr necesse est patrī _____ manēre.

    a. in urbēs   b. urbī   c. in urbe   d. urbium

_____3. The crowd cheered <u>the king</u> as he appeared on the balcony.

    a. rēgī   b. rēgem   c. rēgibus   d. rēge

_____4. _____ prope Circum invenīre nōn poteram.

    a. Tū   b. Is   c. Tē   d. Nōbīs

_____5. He was attacked by men <u>whose</u> crimes had been many.

    a. quārum   b. cuī   c. quōs   d. quōrum

_____6. Dōnā <u>mihi</u> tuam pecūniam!

    a. for me   b. to me   c. mine   d. by me

_____7. Invēnistīne fūrem?

    a. Did you find the thief?   c. Has the thief found you?
    b. You did not find the thief.   d. Will you find the thief?

_____8. Finally, our soldiers <u>began to fight</u> courageously.

    a. pugnāre   b. pugnāverant   c. pugnābant   d. pugnant

_____9. Why must we go <u>across the river</u>?

    a. per flūmina b. in flūminibus c. super flūmen d. trans flūmen

___10. _____, mihi auxilium statim fer!

    a. Servī   b. Serve   c. Servus   d. Servō

___11. Nōbīs multās fābulās <u>dē deīs</u> nārrāvistī.

    a. with the gods b. by the gods c. about the gods d. to the gods

___12. Capiō : _____ :: sum : esse.

    a. capere   b. cēpistis   c. cape   d. capiam

___13. Nōlīte currere per villam, līberī!

    a. The children are not running through the house.
    b. Do run out of the house, children!
    c. Don't run through the house, children!
    d. Don't run into the house, children!!

___ 14. My <u>sister's</u> letter will arrive soon.

    a. soror   b. sorōrum   c. sorōris   d. sorōrēs

___ 15. Hodiē meī parentēs sunt _____ .

    a. īrātus   b. īrātī   c. īrātum   d. īrātōs

___ 16. Fortis : fortiter :: magnus : _____ .

    a. māgnoperē   b. magnē   c. magnum   d. magna

___ 17. Vīgintī minus decem sunt _____ .

    a. decem   b. ūndecim   c. novem   d. trīginta

___ 18. Antōnius _____ ad thermās nōn īverat.

    a. frātrēs   b. dē frātribus   c. frātrem   d. cum frātribus

___ 19. Bēstiārius _____ ferōcem leōnem nōn timet.

    a. fortem   b. fortī   c. fortium   d. fortis

___ 20. Hodiē tū es miser. Crās, fōrtasse, _____ laetus.

    a. eras   b. eris   c. es   d. fueris

PRACTICE FIVE

*Select the best answer from **a**, **b**, **c**, or **d**. Place the letter of your answer in the space provided.*

_____1. _____ fēmina est uxor clārī senatōris.

    a. Hae   b. Hārum   c. Haec   d. Hanc

_____2. Māter fīliam ex hortō <u>magnā vōce</u> vocābit.

    a. of a loud voice   b. in loud voices   c. for a loud voice   d. in a loud voice

_____3. "_____ sunt virī quī in bellō interfectī erant," dīxit Aenēās.

    a. Fēlīcēs   b. Fēlīcī   c. Fēlix   d. Fēlīcem

_____4. By tomorrow, we <u>will have completed</u> all our work for you.

    a. conficiēmus   b. confēcerimus   c. confēcerāmus   d. conficimus

_____5. Eī eam ad iānuam salūtāvērunt.

    a. They greeted him at the door.   c. He had greeted her at the door.
    b. They greeted her at the door.   d. She greeted them at the door.

_____6. Servī in culīnā hortōque _____ diū labōrābant.

    a. dīligentī   b. dīligentōs   c. dīligenter   d. dīligēns

_____7. Tabellārius epistulās <u>to the senator</u> tradidit.

    a. ad senatōrem   b. senatōrēs   c. senatōre   d. senatōrī

_____8. Mox mīlitēs <u>the city</u> appropīnquābunt.

    a. urbī   b. urbem   c. urbibus   d. urbis

_____9. pūniēbat : pūnīverat :: _____ potuerant.

    a. potuerint   b. poterant   c. possunt   d. poterunt

___10. Multī avēs <u>super templa</u> volant.

    a. across the temple   c. into the temples
    b. through the temples   d. over the temples

___11. Dominus et aliī servī _____ in silvā fugītum petēbant.

    a. canēs   b. canī   c. canum   d. cum canibus

___12. Necesse est <u>patrī aut patruō</u> in urbem tēcum īre.

    a. for father or uncle   c. for father and uncle
    b. neither father or uncle   d. for both father and uncle

___ 13. Līberī hominēs et plaustra in viā vīderant.
   a. The children did see men and wagons on the road.
   b. The men had seen children and wagons on the road.
   c. The children had seen men and wagons on the road.
   d. The children and the men had seen the wagons on the road.

___ 14. Students, <u>listen</u> to your teacher!
   a. audīre   b. audīte   c. audī   d. audiunt

___ 15. Cūr tū vestēs <u>in cistā</u> posuistī, ancilla?
   a. in the trunk   b. above the trunks c. near the trunk   d. by the trunk

___ 16. _____ in agrīs diū currere poterant.
   a. Antōnius et soror   c. Antōnium sorōremque
   b. Antōnius   d. Mīlitī

___ 17. Ego sciō illum virum <u>who</u> prope prīncipem stat.
   a. quid   b. quī   c. quis   d. quem

___ 18. Baculum : _____ :: onus : oneris.
   a. baculōrum   b. baculī   c. bacula   d. baculīs

___ 19. Crās vōs in urbem _____.
   a. dūcitis   b. dūxistī   c. dūxeram   d. dūcam

___ 20. Quot rotās habet cisium?
   a. II   b. VI   c. III   d. IX

PRACTICE SIX

Select the best answer from a, b, c, or d. Place the letter of your answer in the space provided.

____1. Helena Paridī <u>ā Venere</u> data est.

    a. with Venus   b. by Venus   c. to Venus   d. for Venus

____2. "Venī _____ ad Circum!" pater fīliō dīxit.

    a. mī   b. mēcum   c. ego   d. mihi

____3. Omnēs sorōrēs sunt _____ .

    a. pulchrae   b. pulchra   c. pulchrās   d. pulchrārum

____4. Volet : voluerit :: _____ : actae eritis.

    a. agēminī   b. agiminī   c. egistis   d. agitis

____5. In ferculō erant olīvae nigrae. Dōnā _____ mihi!

    a. illud   b. illīs   c. illās   d. illae

____6. <u>With great fear</u> Androcles approached the lion.

    a. magnīs timōribus   c. magnum timōrem
    b. magnus timor   d. magnō cum timōre

____7. XL minus XXV sunt _____ .

    a. IV   b. XXXV   c. XV   d. XXV

____8. "_____ , discipulī!" magister puerīs dīxit.

    a. Tacē   b. Tacēte   c. Tacent   d. Tacēre

____9. Ille senātor dē tē in Cūriā <u>bene</u> dīxit.

    a. badly   b. beneficial   c. well   d. good

___10. Coquus multa holera <u>circum porcum</u> posuit.

    a. around the pig   b. inside the pig   c. over the pig   d. under the pig

___11. Nūntius, <u>quī epistulam ad patrem tulerat</u>, nunc valdē dēfessus erat.

    a. whose letter had been brought to father
    b. to whom father has sent the letter
    c. who was bringing the letter to father
    d. who had brought the letter to father

___12. <u>Quō</u> Rōmānae nāvēs nāvigābunt?

    a. From what place   c. To what place
    b. Why   d. For how long

___ 13. Pater iuvenibus praemium _____ parābat.

    a. date   b. dare   c. darī   d. dant

___ 14. Nocte _____ hominēs in viīs urbis nōn vidēbis.

    a. multōrum   b. multōs   c. multīs   d. multī

___ 15. _____ līberōrum audīre mihi placet.

    a. Rīsum   b. Rīsus   c. Rīsuum   d. Rīsū

___ 16. _____ ā fūribus surrepta est.

    a. Carrus   b. Vestīmenta   c. Pecūnia   d. Flōrēs

___ 17. Nōs <u>him</u> prope tabernam laniī occurrēmus.

    a. eum   b. eīs   c. eius   d. eī

___ 18. Discipulī ab ēgregiō magistrō docentur.

    a. The students will be taught by an excellent teacher.
    b. The excellent students will teach the teacher.
    c. The students have been taught by an excellent teacher.
    d. The students are being taught by an excellent teacher.

___ 19. <u>Duōbus diēbus</u> Rōmam pervēnerāmus.

    a. In two days   b. Two days ago   c. After two days   d. For two days

___ 20. Duo servī, <u>to whom</u> mercātor porcum vēndiderat, domum statim festīnāvērunt.

    a. cuī   b. quōs   c. quibus   d. quibuscum

PRACTICE SEVEN

Select the best answer from a, b, c, or d. Place the letter of your answer in the space provided.

_____1. Now the emperor will give the signal <u>to the charioteers</u> to begin the race.

    a. aurīgīs   b. ad aurīgam   c. aurīgās   d. aurīgae

_____2. By tomorrow, <u>they will have seen</u> all the major sites of this city.

    a. vīdērunt   b. vīsī erant   c. vīderint   d. vidēbunt

_____3. Cūr <u>for the army</u> flūmen transīre nōn licet?

    a. exercituum   b. exercituī   c. exercitus   d. exercitibus

_____4. Ego pecūniam <u>to this</u> praedōnī nōn dabō.

    a. huius   b. hoc   c. huic   d. hunc

_____5. Pūniēbās : pūnīre :: _____ posse.

    a. potes   b. potuerās   c. poteris   d. poterās

_____6. Minerva went <u>with Venus and Juno</u> to see Paris.

    a. cum Venere aut Iunōne   c. Venerem et Iunōnem
    b. ā Venere et Iunōne   d. cum Venere Iunōneque

_____7. Īte statim ad cubicula, Claudia et Antōnia!

    a. Don't go for a long time to your rooms, Claudia and Antonia!
    b. Antonia and Claudia, go to your rooms immediately!
    c. Will you go to your room immediately, Claudia and Antonia!
    d. Antonia and Claudia immediately go to their rooms.

_____8. Fidēs : fideī :: strepitūs : _____ .

    a. strepitū   b. strepitum   c. strepituum   d. strepitus

_____9. Num noster coquus hanc cēnam parāvit?

    a. Did our cook prepare this dinner?
    b. Indeed our cook has prepared this dinner.
    c. Our cook didn't prepare this dinner, did he?
    d. Our cook prepared this dinner, didn't he?

___10. _____ tempōre dux auxilium exercituī feret.

    a. Brevī   b. Brevium   c. Brevis   d. Breve

___11. Ego domum <u>without you</u> nōn ībō.

    a. vōs   b. tēcum   c. ā tē   d. sine tē

___12. Hoc bellum ab hostibus <u>acriter</u> pugnātum est.

    a. bitterly   b. rather bitterly   c. very bitter   d. bitter

___ 13. Frūctūs in mensā _____ .

    a. positī sunt   b. positus erat   c. pōnēbāmur   d. pōnī

___ 14. Complūrēs mensēs exercitus in hībernīs fuerat.

    a. a few months ago   c. within several months
    b. for several months   d. after several months

___ 15. Mīlitēs diū _____ mānserant.

    a. ad oppidum   b. oppidōrum   c. in oppida   d. in oppidō

___ 16. Ancilla, cuius stola erat sordida, ā dominā in villam remissa est.

    a. who   b. to which   c. whose   d. what

___ 17. What time of day is it?

    a. diērum   b. dieī   c. diē   d. diēbus

___ 18. LIV plus XLVI sunt _____ .

    a. C   b. XC   c. CXX   d. LXX

___ 19. Sēnsī: sentīre :: _____ : nōlle.

    a. nōn vult   b. nōlet   c. nōluit   d. nōluerat

___ 20. Imperātor haec oppida to be seized cupīvit.

    a. cēpit   b. cape   c. capere   d. capī

LATIN TO ENGLISH VOCABULARY

A

ā, ab, prep. + abl., *away from, by*
accido, -ere, -cidī, —, *to fall upon, to happen*
accipiō, -ere, -cēpī, -ceptus, *to accept*
acer, acris, acre, *bitter, sharp*
acūmen, -inis, n., *keenness; point*
ad, prep. + acc., *to, towards*
admittō, -ere, -mīsī, -missus, *to send to, admit*
adveniō, -īre, -vēnī, -ventus, *to come to, reach, arrive at*
aedificō, -āre, -āvī, -ātus, *to build*
aedificium, -ī, n., *building*
aeger, -gra, -grum, *ill, sick*
Aenēās, -ae, m., *Aeneas*
aequus, -a, -um, *equal*
aestus, -ūs, m., *heat*
aetās, aetātis, f., *youth*
ager, agrī, m., *field*
agō, -ere, ēgī, āctus, *to lead, drive*
   agere grātiās, *to thank*
agricola, -ae, m., *farmer*
Agrippa, -ae, m., *Agrippa*
alacer, -cris, -cre, *lively, quick, glad*
aliī... aliī, *some ... others*
aliquis, aliquid, *someone*
ambulo, -āre, -āvī, -ātus, *to walk*
amīca, -ae, f., *friend*
amīcus, -ī, m., *friend*
amō, -āre, -āvī, -ātus, *to love, to like (to)*
amor, amōris, m., *love*
amphitheātrum, -ī, n., *amphitheater*
ancilla, -ae, f., *handmaiden, maid-servant*
animal, -ālis, n., *animal*
animus, ī, m., *soul*
annus, -ī, m., *year*
Antōnia, -ae, f., *Antonia*
Antōnius, -ī, m., *Antonius*
aperiō, -īre, -uī, -tus, *to uncover, open*
appāreō, -ēre, -uī, -itūrus, *to appear*
appropīnquo, -āre, -āvī, -ātus, *to approach*
aqua, -ae, f., *water*
arbor, -oris, f., *tree*
arcus, -ūs, m., *arch*
ārea, -ae, f. *open space*
arēna, -ae, f., *sand*
arripiō, -ere, -uī, -reptus, *to seize, snatch*

ars, artis, f., *skill, art*
ascendō, -ere, -scendī, -scēnsus, *to climb, ascend*
at, conj., *but*
āter, ātra, ātrum, *black*
Atia, -ae, f., *Atia*
atque, conj., *and*
ātrium, -ī, n., *fore-court, hall*
audāx, -ācis, *bold*
audiō, -īre, -īvī, -ītus, *to hear*
Augustus, -ī, m., *Augustus*
aura, -ae, f., *breeze, wind*
aureus, -a, -um, *of gold, golden*
aurīga, -ae, m./f., *charioteer*
auris, -is, f., *ear*
aut, conj., *or*
   aut ... aut ..., conj., *either...or*
auxilium, ī, n., *help, aid*
avia, -ae, f., *grandmother*
avidus, -a, -um, *eager, greedy*
avis, -is, m./f., *bird*
avunculus, -ī, m., *uncle*
avus, -ī, m., *grandfather*

B

baculum, -ī, n., *stick*
Balbus, -ī, m., *Balbus*
barba, -ae, f., *beard*
barbarus, -a, -um, *barbarian*
bellicus, -a, -um, *of war, military*
bellum, -ī, n., *war*
bene, adv., *well*
bēstiārius, ī, m. *one who fights with wild beasts*
bibliothēca, -ae, f., *library*
bonus, -a, -um, *good*
bōs, bovis, f., *cow*
brāca, -ae, f., *trousers*
bracchium, -ī, n., *arm*
brevis, -e, *brief, short*
Brundisium, -ī, n., *Brundisium*
Brūtus, -ī, m., *Brutus*

C

cadō, -ere, cecidī, casūrus, *to fall down*
caldārium, -ī, n., *hot pool*
calidus, -a, -um, *hot*
Calpurnia, -ae, f., *Capurnia*

Campus Martius, -ī, m., *the Campus Martius*
canis, -is, m./f., *dog*
cantō, -āre, -āvī, -ātus, *to sing*
capiō, -ere, cēpī, captus, *to sieze, capture*
capsa, -ae, f., *a case for books*
captīvus, -a, -um, *captive*, as subst., m., *prisoner*
caput, capitis, n., *head*
careō, carēre, -uī, -itūrus, *to be without, be free from*
carmen, -inis, n., *song, poem*
carō, carnis, f., *flesh*
carrus, -ī, m., *wagon, cart*
Carthāgō, -inis, f., *Carthage*
cārus, -a, -um, *dear*
casa, -ae, f., *hut*
castitās, -ātis, f., *purity, chastity*
caupō, -ōnis, m., *innkeeper*
caveō, -ēre, cāvī, cautus, *to take care, beware*
celer, celeris, celere, *fast, swift*
celeriter, adv., *swiftly*
cēlō, -āre, -āvī, -ātus, *to hide, conceal*
cēna, -ae, f., *dinner*
Cerberus, -ī, m., *Cerberus*
certāmen, -inis, n., *contest, struggle, strife*
cibum, -ī, n., *food*
circum, adv., & prep. + acc., *around*
circus, -ī, m., *circle, race-course*
cisium, ī, n., *a light two-wheeled vehicle*
cista, -ae, f., *trunk, box, basket*
cithara, -ae, f., *cithara, guitar*
   citharā fōrmat, *plays on the cithara*
clāmō, -āre, -āvī, -ātus, *to shout, call*
clāmōr, -ōris, m., *shout, cry*
clārus, -a, -um, *clear*
Claudia, -ae, f., *Claudia*
cliēns, -ntis, m., *client*
cocleare, coclearis, n., *ladle, spoon*
cōgitō, -āre, -āvī, -ātus, *to think*
collum, -ī, n., *neck*
coma, -ae, f., *hair*
commoveō, -ēre, -mōvī, -mōtus, *to disturb, excite*
commūnis, -e, *common, general, public*
compleō, -ēre, -ēvī, -ētus, *to fill up*
complūrēs, -a, pl., *several, many*
cōnficiō, -ere, -fēcī, -fectus, *to prepare, complete*
cōniciō, -ere, -iēcī, -iectus, *to throw together, collect*
coniugium, -ī, n., *marriage*
coniūnx, -iugis, m./f., *a married person, spouse*
cōnsilium, -ī, n., *plan, advice*

cōnsōbrīnus, -ī, m., *cousin*
cōnspiciō, -ere, -spēxī, -spectus, *to look at, observe*
contrā, adv. & prep. + acc., *against, in front, opposite*
contubernium, -ī, n., *company*
cōnūbium, -ī, n., *marriage*
convocō, -āre, -āvī, -ātus, *to call together*
cōpia, -ae, f., *supply (of); (pl.) troops*
coquus, -ī, m., *cook*
corbis, -is, m., *basket*
corpus, -ōris, n., *body*
cotīdiē, adv., *daily*
crās, adv., *tomorrow*
crēdō, -ere, -didi, -ditus, *to trust, believe*
crīnis, -is, m., *hair*
crūs, crūris, n., *leg*
cubiculum, -ī, n., *bedchamber*
cubitum, -ī, n., *elbow*
cubō, -āre, -uī, -itus, *to lie down, recline*
culīna, -ae, f., *kitchen*
cum, conj., *when*
cum, prep. + abl., *with*
cupidus, -a, -um, *desirous (of)*
cupiō, -ere, -īvī, -ītus, *to desire, long for*
cūr, interrog., *why*
cūra, -ae, f., *care, attention*
cūria, -ae, f., *a senate house*
cūrō, -āre, -āvī, -ātus, *to care for, attend to*
currō, -ere, cucurrī, cursus, *to run*
custōdiō, īre, -īvī, -ītus, *to watch guard*

D

dē, prep. + abl., *about, down from*
dea, -ae, f., *goddess*
decem, *ten*
dēcoctor, -ōris, m., *spendthrift, ruined man*
dēfendō, -ere, -fendī, -fēnsus, *to ward off, avert*
dēfessus, -a, -um, *exhausted*
deinde, adv., *then, next*
dēlectō, -āre, -āvī, -ātus, *to delight, charm*
dēleō, -ēre, -ēvī, -ētus, *to destroy, erase*
dēmōnstrō, -āre, -āvī, -ātus, *to point out, show*
dēmum, adv., *at last, finally*
dēnārius, -ī, m., *a silver coin*
dēscendō, -ere, -dī, -sus, *to climb down, descend*
dēsertus, -a, -um, *deserted, solitary*
dētineō, -ēre, -tinuī, -tentus, *to hold off, detain*
deus, -ī, m., *god*
dīcō, -ere, dīxī, dictus, *to say, speak, tell*

Dīdō, Dīdōnis f., *Dido*
diēs, -ēī, m., *day*
difficilis, -e, *difficult*
digitus, -ī, m., *finger*
dīgnus, -a, -um + abl., *worthy, deserving*
dīligēns, -ntis, *careful, diligent*
dīligenter, adv., *diligently*
Dīs, Dītis, m., *Dis, god of the underworld*
discēdō, -ere, -cessī, -cessus, *to divide, scatter, tear apart*
discernō, -ere, -crēvī, -crētus, *to separate, divide*
dīscindō, -ere, -cidī, -cissus, *to tear asunder, cut apart*
discipulus, -ī, m., *student*
discrētus, -a, -um, *hidden*
dispōnō, -ere, -posuī, -positus, *to place, distribute, arrange*
diū, adv., *for a long time*
dō, dare, dedī, datus, *to give*
doceō, -ēre, -uī, -tus, *to teach*
dolōrōsus, -a, -um, *causing anxiety, painful*
dominus, -ī, m., *master*
domus, -ūs, f., *home*
dōnō -āre, -āvī, -ātus, *to give*
dormiō, -īre, -īvī, -ītus, *to sleep*
dūcō, dūcere, dūxī, ductus, *to lead*
dulcis, -e, *sweet*
dum, adv., *while*
duo, -ae, -o, *two*
dūrus, -a, -um, *tough, hard*
dux, ducis, m., *leader*

E

ē, ex, prep. + abl., *out of*
ēdiscō, -ere, edidicī, —, *to learn thoroughly, commit to memory*
ēdō, -ere, didī, -ditus, *to eat*
ēdūcō, -ere, -dūxī, -ductus, *to lead forth, draw out*
efficiō, -ere, -fēcī, -fectus, *to bring to pass, cause*
effugiō, -ere, -fūgī, —, *to flee away, escape*
ego, *I*
ēgregius, -a, -um, *outstanding, distinguished*
ēlegans, -antis, *delicate, elegant*
Elissa, -ae, f., *Dido*
emō, -ere, ēmī, ēmptus, *to buy*
eō, īre, īvī, ītus, *to go*
epistula, -ae, f., *letter*
equus, -ī, m., *horse*
errō, -āre, -āvī, -ātus, *to wander, roam*
ērudītus, -a, -um, *educated, learned*

etiam, adv., *now, even, yet*
ēveniō, -īre, -vēnī, -ventus, *to come out, happen*
ēventum, -ī, n., *occurrence, event*
ēventus, -ūs, m., *outcome, fate, event*
excipiō, -ere, -cēpī, -ceptus, *to take out, withdraw*
excītō, -āre, -āvī, -ātus, *to stir up, excite*
exercitus, -ūs, m., *army*
explōrātor, -ōris, m., *explorer, spy*
exsilium, -ī, n., *exile, banishment*
exspectō, -āre, -āvī, -ātus, *to await, expect*
extrā, adv. & prep. + abl., *outside of, beyond*

F

fābula, -ae, f., *story*
faciēs, -ēī, f., *appearance, face*
facilis, -e, *easy*
faciō, -ere, fēcī, factus, *to make, do*
fāma, -ae, f., *rumor, reputation*
familia, -ae, f., *household*
fēlīx, -īcis, *happy, lucky; fruitful*
fēmina, -ae, f., *woman*
ferculum, -ī, n., *serving tray*
ferō, ferre, tulī, lātus, *to bear, carry, bring*
ferōcia, -ae, f., *wildness, fierceness*
ferōciter, adv., *fiercely, boldly*
ferōx, -ōcis, *fierce, bold, wild*
festīnō, -āre, -āvī, -ātus, *to hasten, hurry*
fidēlis, -e, *trustworthy, faithful*
fidēs, -ēī, f., *pledge, trust*
fīlia, -ae, f., *daughter*
fīlius, -ī, m., *son*
fīniō, -īre, īvī, -ītus, *to finish*
fīnis, -is, m., *end, boundary, limit*
flōs, flōris, m., *flower*
flūmen, flūminis, n., *river*
fōrmō, -āre, -āvī, -ātus, *to shape, form, build*
fōrtasse, adv., *perhaps*
fortis, -e, *brave, strong*
fortūnātus, -a, -um, *fortunate*
forum, -ī, n., *a forum, marketplace*
Forum, -ī, n., *the Forum in Rome*
fossa, -ae, f., *ditch, trench*
fragor, fragōris, m., *crash*
frangō, -ere, frēgī, frāctus, *to break*
frāter, -tris, m., *brother*
frīgidārium, -ī, n., *cold pool*
frūctus, -ūs, m., *fruit*
frūgālitās, -tātis, f., *thriftiness, economy, frugality*
frūmentum, -ī, n., *grain*
frūstrā, adv., *in vain, for nothing*

fugiō, -īre, -īvī, -ītus, *to flee*
fugitīvus, -a, -um, *futugive*
fundō, fundere, fūdī, fūsus, *to pour out*
fūr, fūris, m., *thief*
furnus, -ī, m., *oven*

G

gaudium, -ī, n., *joy*
gemma, -ae, f., *gem, jewel*
genetrīx, -īcis, f., *a mother*
gerō, -ere, gessī, gestus, *to bear, carry, wear, hold*
gladiātor, -ōris, m., *gladiator*
gladius, -ī, m., *sword*
Graecia, -ae, f., *Greece*
Graecus, -a, -um, *Greek*
grātia, -ae, f., *favor, esteem, regard*
grātus, -a, -um, *dear, pleasing*
gravis, -e, *heavy, serious*
Gryneus, -a, -um, *of Gryneus*

H

habēna, -ae, f., *halter, rein*
habeō, -ēre, -uī, -itus, *to have, hold*
habitō, -āre, -āvī, -ātus, *to dwell, live*
haereō, -ēre, haesī, haesūrus, *to hang, stick, cling*
herī, adv., *yesterday*
heu, interjection, *alas*
hībernus, -a, -um, *of winter*, as subst., n., *winter-quarters*
hic, haec, hoc, *this*
hīc, adv., *here*
hinc, adv., *from this place*
hodiē, adv., *today*
holus, -eris, n., *vegetables*
homō, hominis, m., *man*
honestum -ī, n., *honesty, integrity*
honestus, -a,-um, *respected, honored, distinguished, noble*
hōra, -ae, f., *hour*
hortus, -ī, m., *garden*
hostis, -is, m., *enemy*

I

iaceō, -ēre, uī, —, *to lie, be situated*
iam, adv., *now, already*
iānua, -ae, f., *door*
ibi, adv., *there*
īdolon, -ī, n., *image, ghost*

ientāculum, -ī, n., *breakfast*
igitur, conj., *therefore*
īgnāvus, -a, -um, *lazy*
ille, illa, illum, *that*
imāgō, -inis, f., *image, likeness, ghost*
imperātōr, -ōris, m., *commander, general*
in, prep. + abl., *in, on;* prep. + acc., *in, into*
incendium, -ī, n., *fire*
incipiō, -ere, -cēpī, -ceptus, *to begin*
incitō, -āre, -āvī, -ātus, *to arouse, incite*
incola, -ae, m., *tenant, inhabitant*
inde, adv., *from that place*
indulgeō, -ēre, -ulsī, -ultus, *to be kind, yield, allow*
induō, -ere, -uī, -ūtus, *to put on, assume*
īnfacētus, -a, -um, *without wit, stupid*
īnfāmis, -e, *notorious, disreputable*
īnfāns, īnfantis, m./f., *infant*
īnfēlīx,-īcis, *unfruitful, barren*
ingēns, -ntis, *huge; natural*
inquit (defect.), *he, she says*
īnsānus, -a, -um, *insane, mad*
insapiens, -ntis, *unwise*
īnsula, -ae, f., *island, apartment*
intellegō, -ere, -lēxī, -lēctus, *to come to know, understand*
intelligēns, -ntis, *intelligent*
interdiū, adv., *during the day*
interficiō, -ere, -fēcī, -fectus, *to kill*
intrō, -āre, āvī, -ātus, *to enter*
intus, adv., *on the inside, within*
inveniō, -īre, -vēnī, -ventus, *to come upon, find*
invitō, -āre, -āvī, -ātus, *to invite*
ipse, ipsa, ipsum, *himself, herself*
īra, -ae, f., *anger*
īrāscor, -ī, īrātus sum, *to be angry*
īrātus, -a, -um, *angry*
is, ea, id, *he, she, it; this, that*
ita, conj., *so*
Ītalia, -ae, f., *Italy*
itaque, conj., *therefore*
iter, itineris, n., *journey*
iterum, adv., *again, once more*
iubeō, -ēre, iussī, iūssus, *to order, command*
iūdex, -icis, m., *judge*
iūdicium, -ī, n., *judgment, decision*
Iūlia, -ae, f., *Julia*
Iūlius, -ī, m., *Julius*
Iūnō, -ōnis, f., *The goddess Juno*
iurō, -āre, -āvī, -ātus, *to swear*
iūs, iūris, n., *soup*

L

labor, -ōris, m., *labor, toil, work*
labōrō, -āre, -āvī, -ātus, *to work, labor*
lacrimō, -āre, -āvī, -ātus, *to cry, weep*
laetus, -a, -um, *happy*
lāna, -ae, f., *wool*
   lānam trahere, *to spin wool*
lanius, -ī, m., *butcher*
lātrātus, -ūs, m., *barking*
lātrō, -āre, -āvī, -ātus, *to bark*
lātus, -a, -um, *wide*
laudō, -āre, –āvī, -ātus, *to praise*
lavō, -āre, -āvī, -ātus, *to wash*
lectīca, -ae, f., *litter, sedan*
lēctitō, -āre, -āvī, -ātus, *to read often, recite*
lectus, -ī, m., *bed*
legō, -ere, lēgī, lēctus, *to read, choose*
lentus, -a, um, *slow*
leō, -ōnis, m., *lion*
lex, lēgis, f., *law*
libellus, -ī, m., *little book*
liber, -brī, m., *book*
līber, -era, -erum, *free*
līberī, -ōrum, m. pl., *children*
licet, licēre, licuit, *to allow, to permit*
lītus, -ōris, n., *seashore*
locus, -ī, m., *place*
longus, -a, -um, *long*
lūceō, -ēre, lūxī, —, *to be light, shine*
lūdus, -ī, m., *school, game*
lupus, -ī, m., *wolf*
Lycia, -ae, f., *country of Asia*

M

macellum, -ī, n., *butcher's stall, meat-market*
maestus, -a, -um, *sad*
magis, comp. adv., *more*
magister, -strī, m., *teacher*
magistra, ae, f., *teacher*
māgnificus, -a, -um, *great, noble, distinguished*
māgnopere, adv., *greatly*
māgnus, -a, -um, *large*
mālum, -ī, n., *apple*
malus, -a, -um, *bad*
mandātum, -ī, n., *order*
mandō, -āre, -āvī, -ātus, *to entrust (to), order*
manē, adv., *in the morning, early*
maneō, -ēre, -sī, mānsus, *to remain*
manus, -ūs, f., *hand*
mappa, -ae, f., *napkin*

Marcellus, -ī, m., *Marcellus*
marītus, -a, -um, *of marriage, conjugal, nuptial;* as subst., m., *husband*
marītus, -ī, m., *husband*
māter, -tris, f., *mother*
mātrimōnium, -ī, n., *wedlock, marriage*
   in mātrimōnium dūcere, *to marry*
māximus, -a, -um, *greatest*
memoria, -ae, f., *memory*
mēnsa, -ae, f., *table, desk*
mēnsis, -is, m., *month*
mercātor, -ōris, m., *trader, merchant*
meus, -a, -um, *mine, my*
mīles, -itis, m., *soldier*
Minerva, -ae, f., *The goddess Minerva*
minimus, -a, -um, *least*
minor, minus, *younger*
mīrus, -a, -um, *wonderful*
miser, -era, -erum, *wretched, miserable*
mittō, -ere, mīsī, missus, *to send*
molestus, -a, um, *troublesome, grievous*
moneō, -ēre, -uī, -itus, *to warn*
mōns, -ntis, m., *mountain*
   Mōns Palātīnus, *the Palatine Hill*
mōnstrō, -āre, -āvī, -ātus, *to show*
mōnstrum, -ī, n., *warning*
mordeō, -ēre, momordī, morsus, *to bite*
mors, mortis, f., *death*
mortuus, -a, -um, *dead*
moveō, -ēre, mōvī, mōtus, *to move*
mox, adv., *soon*
multus, -a, -um, *many, much*
mūniō, -īre, -īvī, -ītus, *to fortify*
mūnus, -eris, n., *gift, gladiatorial show*
mūs, mūris, m./f., *mouse*

N

nārrō, āre, -āvī, -ātus, *to tell, narrate*
nāsus, -ī, m., *nose*
natō, -āre, -āvī, -ātus, *to swim*
nātūra, -ae, f., *birth, nature*
nauta, -ae, m., *sailor*
nāvigō, -āre, -āvī, -ātus, *to sail*
nāvis, -is, f., *ship*
necesse esse, *to be necessary*
necō, -āre, -āvī, -ātus, *to kill*
nepōs, -ōtis, m., *grandson*
niger, -gra, -grum, *black*
nihil, n. indecl., *nothing*
noctē, adv., *at night*
nōlō, nōlle, nōluī, —, *to wish...not, to be unwilling*
nōmen, -inis, n., *name*

nōn, adv., *not*

nōnne, interrog. adv., *(in a question expecting a 'yes' answer) not?*

nōs, *we*

noster, -tra, -trum, *our*

novem, *nine*

novus, -a, -um, *new, recent*

nox, noctis, f., *night*

nūllus, -a, -um, *not any, no, none*

num, interrog. adv., *(in a question expecting a 'no' answer)*

nūmen, -inis, n., *nod, command, divine will*

numerus, -ī, m., *number*

numquam, adv., *never*

nunc, adv., *now*

nūntiō, -āre, -āvī, -ātus, *to announce*

nūntius, -ī, m., *messenger, message*

nūtrīx, -īcis, f., *nurse, nanny*

O

ōbēsus, -a, -um, *fat, plump*

obstipēscō, -ere, obstipuī, —, *to be dazed, astounded*

occurrō, -ere, -currī, -ursus, *to meet, to run into*

ocellus, -ī, m., *little eye*

Octāvia, ae, f., *Octavia*

Octāvius, -ī, m., *Octavius*

octō, *eight*

oculus, -ī, m., *eye*

ōlim, adv., *one day, once upon a time*

olīva, -ae, f., *olive*

omnis, -e, *all, every*

onus, eris, n., *load, burden*

oppidum, -ī, n., *town*

optimus, -a, -um, *best*

ōrāculum, -ī, n., *oracle, prophecy*

ōrātiō, -ōnis, f., *speech, oration*

ōrātōr, -ōris, m., *speaker*

ōrnāmentum, -ī, n., *apparatus, equipment, furniture, decoration*

ōrnō, -āre, -āvī, -ātus, *to furnish, provide*

ōrō, -āre, -āvī, -ātus, *to beg*

ostendō, -ere, -dī, -tus, *to show, exhibit*

ōvum, -ī, n., *egg*

P

paedagōgus, -ī, m., *governor, preceptor, tutor*

paene, adv., *almost*

palaestra, -ae, f., *place of exercise*

pānis, -is m., *bread*

parēns, -ntis, m./f., *parent*

Paris, -idis, m., *Paris*

parō, -āre, -āvī, -ātus, *to prepare, get ready*

pars, -rtis, f., *part (of)*

parvus, -a, -um, *small*

pāstor, -ōris, m., *herdsman, shepherd*

pater, -tris, m., *father*

patruus, -ī, m., *uncle*

paucī, -ae, -a, *few, a few*

paulisper, adv., *for a little while*

pauper, -peris, *poor, as subst., m, poor man*

pavīmentum, -ī, n., *level surface, hard floor*

pecūnia, -ae, f., *money*

pecus, -oris, n., *cattle*

pellō, -ere, pepulī, pulsus, *to push*

per, prep. + acc., *through*

perfidus, -a, -um, *faithless, perfidious, wicked*

perīculōsus, -a, -um, *wicked*

perīculum, -ī, n., *danger*

peristȳlum, -ī, n., *open court*

permoveō, -ēre, -mōvī, -mōtus, *to move thoroughly*

pernoctō, -āre, -āvī, -ātus, *to stay all night*

perterreō, -ēre, -uī, -itus, *to frighten thoroughly, terrify*

perveniō, -īre, vēnī, -ventus, *to arrive*

pestilēns, -ntis, *infected, unhealthy*

petō, -ere, -īvī, -ītus, *to seek, beg, find*

pictūra, -ae, f., *picture*

pīnguis, -e, *fat*

pīrāta, -ae, m., *pirate*

piscīna, -ae, f.

placidē, adv., *softly, quietly*

plaustrum, -ī, n., *wagon, cart*

plēnus,-a, -um, *full (of)*

plūs, plūris, *much, many*

poena, -ae, f., *punishment, penalty*

poēta, -ae, m., *poet*

pōnō, -ere, posuī, positus, *to put, place*

popīna, -ae, f., *bar*

populus, -ī, m., *people*

porcus, -ī, m., *pig*

porta, -ae, f., *gate*

portō, -āre, -āvī, -ātus, *to carry*

possum, posse, potuī, —, *to be able, can*

post, adv. & prep. +acc., *after*

postulō, -āre, -āvī, -ātus, *to demand*

potēns, ntis, *powerful*

potestās, -ātis, f., *power, authority*

praeclārus, -a, -um, *famous*

praedō, -ōnis, m., *robber*

praemium, -ī, n., *reward*

prīmus, -a, -um, *first*

prīnceps, -ipis, *foremost, first in order, as subst., m., emperor*

prō, prep. + abl., *for, in front of*
procāx, -ācis, *bold, insolent, wanton*
prōmissus, -a, -um, *hanging down, long*
prōmittō, -ere, -mīsī, -missus, *to let go, promise*
prope, adv. & prep. + acc., *near, close*
prōvincia, -ae, f., *province*
prūdēns, -ntis, *wise, knowing*
puella, -ae, f., *girl*
puer, -ī, m., *boy*
pugna, -ae, f., *fight, battle*
pugnō, -āre, -āvī, -ātus, *to fight*
pulcher, -chra, -chrum, *beautiful*
pūniō, -īre, -īvī, -ītus, *to punish*

Q

quaestiō, -ōnis, f., *questioning, inquiry*
quam, adv., *how*
quamdiū, adv., *how long*
quandō, interrog., *when?*
quatiō, -ere, quassī, quassus, *to shake*
quattuor, *four*
quī, quae, quod, *who, which*
quīnque, *five*
quis, quid, interrog., *who?*
quisque, quaeque, *each*
quō, adv., *to what place*
quod, conj., *because*
quōmodo, adv., *how*
quoque, conj., *also*
quot, *how many?*

R

raeda, -ae, f., *wagon*
rāmus, -ī, m., *branch*
recēdō, -ere, -cessī, -cessus, *to go back, withdraw, depart*
recitō, -āre, -āvī, -ātus, *to recite*
rēctus, -a, -um, *straight, upright*
redeō, -īre, -īvī, -ītus, *to return*
regīna, -ae f., *queen*
regiō, -ōnis, f., *territory, region*
regnum, -ī, n., *kingdom*
regō, -ere, rēxī, rēctus, *to rule*
relinquō, -ere, -līquī, -līctus, *to abandon*
reprehendō, -ere, -dī, -sus, *to hold back, seize*
rēs, reī f., *thing, matter*
respiciō, -ere, -spēxī, spectus, *to look back*
respondeō, -ere, -dī, -sum, *to respond, answer*
revēniō, -īre, --vēnī, -ventus, *to return*
revocō, -āre, -āvī, -ātus, *to call back*
rēx, rēgis, m., *king*

rīdeō, -ēre, -sī, -sus, *to laugh*
rīpa -ae, f., *riverbank*
rīsus, -ūs, m., *laughter, smile*
rīvus, -ī, m., *stream*
Rōma, -ae, f., *Rome*
Rōmānus, -a, -um, *Roman*
rota, -ae, f., *wheel*

S

saeclum, ī, n., *race, generation, age*
saepe, adv., *often*
saliō, -īre, -uī, saltus, *to leap, jump*
salūtō, -āre, -āvī, -ātus, *to greet*
salvē, adv., *well, be in good health*
salveō, -ēre, —, —, *to be well*
sapientia, -ae, f., *wisdom*
saxum, -ī, n., *rock, boulder*
scelestus, -a, -um, *impious, wicked*
schola, -ae, f., *hall*
sciō, -ere, scīvī, scītus, *to know*
scrībō, -ere, scrīpsī, scrīptus, *to write*
sed modo, conj., *but also*
sed, conj., *but*
sedeō, -ēre, sēdī, sessus, *to sit*
semper, adv., *always*
senātor, -ōris, m., *senator*
senex, senis, m., *old man*
sentiō, -īre, sēnsī, sēnsus, *to feel, perceive*
septem, *seven*
sērō, adv., *late*
servula, -ae, f., *slave girl, handmaiden*
servus, -ī, m., *slave, servant*
sex, *six*
sīc, adv., *so, thus*
siccus, -a, -um, *dry*
Siculus, -a, -um, *Sicilian*
sīgnum, -ī, n., *mark, sign*
silentium, -ī, n., *silence*
silvae, -ae, f., *forest*
similis, -e, *like, similar*
sine, prep. + abl., *without*
socius, -ī, m., *ally, friend*
sōl, sōlis, m., *sun*
sōleō, -ēre, solitus sum, *to be accustomed*
sollicitus, -a, -um, *agitated, disturbed, troubled*
sōlus, -a, -um, *alone*
somnus, ī, m., *sleep*
sonitus, -ūs, m., *sound*
sordidus, -a, -um, *dirty, filthy*
soror, -ōris, f., *sister*
sors, -tis, f., *oracle, lot*
spatiōsus, -a, -um, *spacious*

speciēs, -ēī f., *sight, kind*
spectāculum, -ī, n., *spectator's seat*
spectō, -āre, -āvī, -ātus, *to see, watch*
speculum, -ī, n., *mirror*
spēs, -ēī, f., *hope*
spōns, -ntis, f., *free will, wish*
stadium, -ī, n., *running track*
statim, adv., *immediately*
statua, ae, f., *statue*
stilus, -ī, m., *pointed instrument*
stō, stāre, stetī, stātus, *to stand*
stola, -ae, f., *gown, stole, dress*
strēnuus, -a, -um, *quick, strenuous*
strepitus, -ūs, m., *noise, crash, clattering*
studium, -ī, n., *zeal*
sub, prep. + abl., *under*
subitō, adv., *immediately, suddenly*
sum, esse, fuī, futūrus, *to be*
summus, -a, -um, *highest*
super, prep. + acc., *over, above*
superō, -āre, -āvī, -ātus, *to overcome*
surgō, -ere, surrēxī, surrectus, *to rise, arise*
surripiō, -ere, -uī, -reptus, *to snatch away, steal*

T

tabellārius, -a, -um, *of a ballot, relating to voting, as subst., m., courier, messenger*
taberna, -ae, f., *shop, tavern*
tablīnum, -ī, n., *dining room*
taceō, -ēre, -uī, -itus, *to be silent*
tam, conj., *so*
tardus, -a, -um, *slow*
temerārius, -a, -um, *rash, thoughtless*
templum, -ī, n., *temple*
temptō, -āre, -āvī, -ātus, *to try, attempt*
tempus, -ōris, n., *time*
teneō, -ēre, -uī, -tus, *to hold*
tepidārium, -ī, n., *warm pool*
ter, adv., *three times*
tergum, -ī, n., *back*
terra, -ae, f., *earth, ground*
terreō, -ēre, -uī, -itus, *to frighten, terrify*
thermae, -ārum, f. pl., *baths*
tigris, -idis, m., *tiger*
timeō, -ēre, -uī, —, *to fear*
timidus, -a, -um, *shy, timid*
timor, -ōris, m., *fear, dread*
toga, -ae, f., *toga*
tōtus, -a, -um, *all, the whole*
trādō, -ere, -didī, -ditus, *to hand over*
trahō, -ere, trāxī, trāctus, *to draw, drag*
trans, prep. + acc., *across*

transeō, -īre, -īvī, -ītus, *to go across*
trēs, trium, *three*
trīclīnium, ī, n., *eating-couch*
trīginta, *thirty*
trīstis, -e, *sad*
Trōia, -ae, f., *Troy*
Trōiānus, -a, -um, *Trojan*
tū, *you*
tumultus, -ūs, m., *commotion*
tunica, -ae, f., *tunic*
turba, -ae, f., *crowd, commotion*
tuus, -a, -um, *yours*

U

ubī, interrog., *where?*
ūltimus, -a, -um, *farthest*
umquam, adv., *ever*
unde, adv., *from what place*
ūndecim, *eleven*
ūnus, -a, -um, *one, single*
urbis, -is, f., *city*
ūsus, -ūs, m., *use, advantage*
uxor, -ōris, f., *wife*

V

valdē, adv., *strongly, intensely*
valeō, -ēre, -uī, -itūrus, *to be strong, be able*
validus, -a, -um, *strong, powerful, able*
vastō, -āre, -āvī, -ātus, *to destroy*
vehemēns, -ntis, *violent, vehement*
vēlōx, -ōcis, *swift, quick*
vēlum, -i, n., *sail, curtain*
vendō, -ere, -didī, -ditus, *to sell*
veniō, -īre, vēnī, ventus, *to come*
Venus, -eris, f., *the goddess Venus*
verberō, -āre, -āvī, -ātus, *to beat, strike*
verbum, -ī, n., *word*
veritās, -ātis, f., *truth*
vērum, -ī, n., *truth*
vērus, -a, -um, *true*
vester, -tra, -trum, *yours (pl.)*
vestīmentum, -ī, n., *clothing*
vestis, -is, f., *garment*
vetus, -eris, *old, aged*
vexō, -āre, -āvī, -ātus, *to shake, harass*
via, -ae, f., *road, way*
Via Appia, -ae, f., *the Appian Way*
vīcīna, -ae, f., *neighborhood, vicinity*
vīcīnus, -a, -um, *neighboring, near*
vīctōria, -ae, f., *victory*
videō, -ēre, vīdī, vīsus, *to see, perceive*
vīgintī, *twenty*

vīlicus, -ī, m., *steward, overseer*
villa, -ae, f., *farmhouse, villa*
vincō, -ere, vīcī, vīctus, *to conquer, defeat*
vinculum, -ī, n., *chain*
vīnum, -ī, n., *wine*
vir, -ī, m., *man*
virga, -ae, f., *rod, switch, stick*
virtūs, -ūtis, f., *manliness, courage*

vīsitō, -āre, -āvī, -ātus, *to visit*
vix, adv., *scarcely*
vocō, -āre, -āvī, -ātus, *to call*
volō, velle, voluī, *to wish*
vōs, *you (pl.)*
vōx, vōcis, f., *voice*
vulnus, -eris, n., *wound*